THE PLEASURES OF HOME
SOFT FURNISHINGS

THE PLEASURES OF HOME
SOFT FURNISHINGS
HILARY MORE

CASSELL

First edition 1998 by
Cassell
Wellington House
125 Strand
London WC2R 0BB

Distributed in the United States
by Sterling Co., Inc.
387 Park Avenue South
New York, NY 10016-8810

British Library Cataloguing-in-Publication-Data
A catalogue record of this book is available from the British Library

ISBN 0-304-34629-2 (hardback)
ISBN 0-304-35091-5 (paperback)

Designed by Blackjacks Limited
Illustrated by Kate Simunek
Picture research by Julia Pashley

Printed and bound in Spain

Contents

Introduction

*F*abric is an indispensable element in an interior design scheme. Used with confidence and flair, it can transform the look of a room. Yet soft furnishings never exist in isolation: they are always seen in the context of their surroundings – the architecture of the home and the style of the room. Whether you are starting from scratch and redecorating a whole room, or are adding to an existing scheme, the style of the room is your starting point.

This book is structured with that fact in mind. Rather than grouping, say, all the curtains together in a chapter, this book presents every project as part of a style to which it is especially well suited. And each chapter consists of a number of projects which will help to create that distinctive style. You won't have to search to find out how to make a particular item of soft furnishing suited to a chosen style, nor will you find yourself wondering just how you can achieve a certain look. The result is a much more inspiring and user-friendly guide to soft furnishings.

The full range of soft furnishings is included, with step-by-step instructions and diagrams for every project. All of the projects can, of course, be adapted, so if you see something in the Cottage Bedroom chapter which you feel would look right in a Gustavian hall, there is no reason why you cannot use it in that way. Similarly, if you love, say, the colonial look but would prefer to use it in the living room, the projects can easily be adapted.

In addition, each book in this series is structured in the same way, so if you feel that, say, colourwashed walls or stencilling would go well with your new Provencal style curtains, just turn to the Provencal Kitchens chapter in those books for full details.

At the beginning of each chapter, there is a short introduction to the style, briefly explaining it in historical or cultural terms, and outlining the basic features of the style. At the beginning of the book, the Basic Techniques section sets out the techniques that are used often in the projects.

Whichever style of decor you prefer, you'll find in these pages a unique blend of inspiration and practical advice.

MILES DAVIS

Basic Techniques

The projects in this book are not difficult; you only need basic sewing skills to do them. The main techniques you will use are explained in this section.

Equipment

To make your own soft furnishings, you need a large, flat, clean work surface – preferably not a carpeted floor – for cutting out fabric. It's a good idea to protect the surface with a cloth or brown parcel paper.

The equipment you will need for sewing these projects includes:

- A sewing machine
- Pins, needles
- A large pair of scissors for cutting out, and a small pair for snipping threads. (Never use these on paper, or they will quickly become blunt.)
- A long metal retractable measure (for curtains), a small, soft measuring tape (for corners and curves) and a metre rule (yardstick)
- An iron
- Tailor's chalk, dressmaker's carbon paper and tracing wheel

Materials

In addition to fabric, you will need the following materials for some or all of the projects:
- Thread: Try to match the fibre as well as the colour – cotton thread for cotton fabric, synthetic thread for synthetic fabric, silk thread for silk fabric. If possible, use lightweight thread for sheer fabric, muslin, voile, etc, and strong thread for heavy fabrics.
- Zips: Again, try to match not only the colour but also the fibre – a natural-fibre zip for cotton, linen, etc, and a synthetic-fibre zip for synthetics.
- Touch-and-close tape such as Velcro: This consists of two strips, one with "hooks" and one with "loops" which interlock when pressed together and separate when pulled apart. It is available in various widths and in sew-on or stick-on versions (or a combination of the two).
- Curtain heading tapes: These are sewn to the top of the curtain then pulled up to form gathers, pencil pleats, triple pleats, box pleats, a smocked effect or various other headings.
- Curtain accessories: A variety of curtain accessories is available including lead curtain weights, leadweight tape and cord tidies.

Flat seams

The most commonly used seam for most kinds of sewing is the flat seam.

1 With right sides together and raw edges even, pin the two pieces of fabric together, matching any pattern, and placing the pins at right angles to the edges.

2 If you are easing a curved edge onto a straight edge, or if you are a beginner, tack just inside the seamline and remove pins. Otherwise, you can leave the pins in and either stitch over them or remove them as you go, depending on what your sewing machine manual advises.

3 Stitch along the seamline specified in the instructions – generally 1.5cm (⅝in) from the edge.

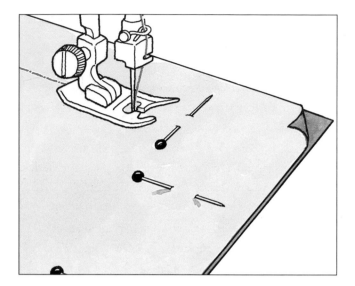

4 To sew around a corner, stop the stitching when you reach the next seamline. With the needle in the fabric, lift the presser foot and turn the fabric until the new seamline is in line with the presser foot. Now lower the presser foot and continue stitching. If it is a very sharp corner and the fabric is bulky, stitch two stitches across the point.

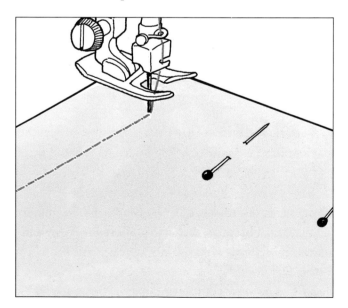

5 At each end, either work a few stitches in reverse, or tie the threads by hand. (If the seam does not finish at any edge, you need to pull one thread back and insert a pin into the loop at its base and pull the second thread through, before tying it.)

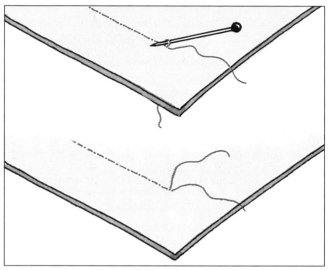

6 Remove any tacking threads or any remaining pins and press the seam open. Finally, trim the seam, clip any corners and curves, or neaten the raw edges, as explained overleaf.

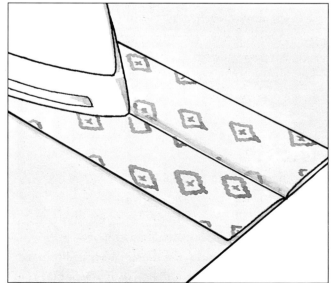

Seam allowances

For an outer corner, cut off the point of the seam allowance on both layers. For an inner corner, clip into the seam allowance (but not into the stitching) at the corner. If you don't do this the corner will not be smooth and flat.

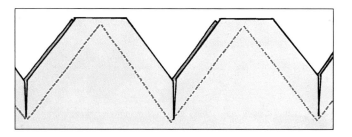

For curves, clip into the seam allowance to make the seam lie flat. (For inward curves, cut narrow V-shapes.)

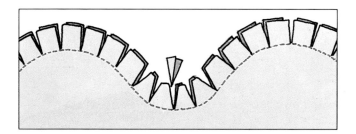

For a seam with several layers, "grade" or "layer" the seam by trimming each layer to a different width.

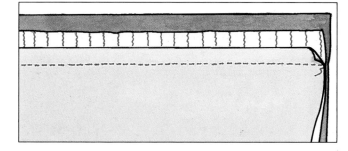

On curtains, selvedges should be trimmed off or clipped at intervals, otherwise they can cause puckering.

Zigzag stitching each raw edge of a seam allowance is a quick way of neatening them so they won't fray.

Flat-fell seam

This type of seam is strong and hard-wearing. It is used on unlined curtains. A row of stitching shows from the right side of the fabric.

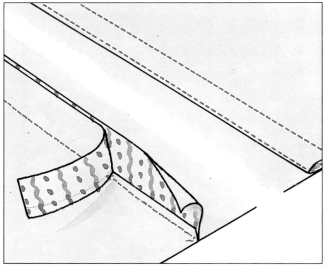

1 With right sides together, stitch the seam in the usual way along the seamline. Trim one edge to within 6mm (1/4in) of the stitching line. Press the seam so that the wider seam allowance is on top of the narrower one.

2 Fold the wider seam allowance in half, enclosing the narrower one, and pin it to the fabric. Stitch along the folded edge parallel to the previous stitching line.

French seam

Use this for sheer fabrics.

1 With *wrong* sides together and raw edges even, pin and stitch the seam parallel to the ultimate seamline but within the seam allowance. For example, if the seam allowance allowed for in the instructions is 1.5cm (5/8in), you should stitch 5mm (1/4in) from the raw edge. Press the seam open.

2 Turn the fabric back on itself so that the right sides are together and the seamline you've just stitched runs along the fold. Pin and stitch along the ultimate seamline, enclosing the raw edges of the previous seam. In the example in step 1, you would be stitching 1cm (³/₈in) from the foldline. Press the new seam allowance to one side.

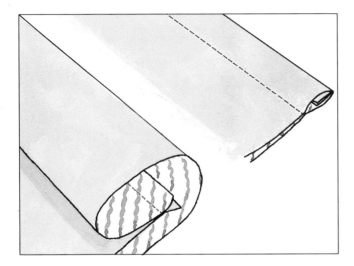

Mitred corners

Mitring eliminates bulk to make a neat, flat corner. There are different techniques for different types of corner.

To mitre a corner where two single hems will meet, turn in both raw edges along the hemlines and press. Use pins to mark the two points where the edges meet. Unfold the hems. Now fold the corner diagonally from

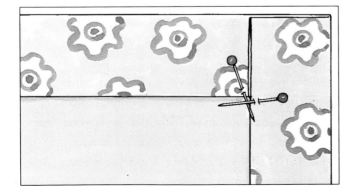

pin to pin; press. Remove the pins. If the fabric is bulky, trim off the corner to within 6mm (¹/₄in) of the diagonal fold. Refold the hems, and slipstitch the edges of the mitre together.

To mitre a corner where two double hems meet, press in the double hems along both edges, then unfold one hem on each side, leaving the other one on each side folded. Mark the points where the edges meet with pins and proceed as for single hems.

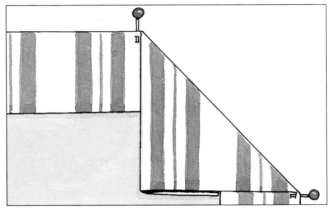

To mitre braid that you are attaching to fabric, stitch along the outer edge to the bottom, and fasten off. Fold the braid back on itself, finger-pressing the fold. Lift the folded end of the braid and handsew a diagonal seam, beginning at the crease. If the braid is bulky, trim off the corner. Now position the braid along the new edge and continue stitching the outer edge. When all the corners are mitred you can stitch the inner edge.

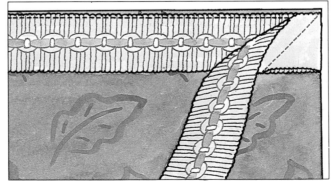

Bias binding

You can buy prefolded bias binding, but if you want a perfect match or an unusual width, you will need to make your own.

1 Establish how wide the binding will be; the strips will need to be four times this width. Fold over the fabric corner so it is even with the adjacent edge.

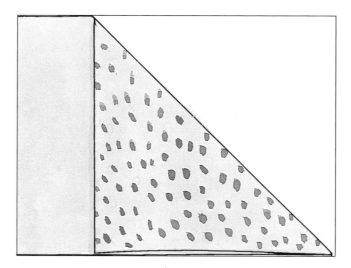

2 Press this diagonal fold. Mark lines parallel to this fold as far apart as the required width of the strips. Cut out along the lines.

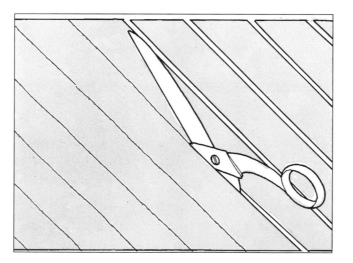

3 Join the ends of the strips on the straight grain (ie with diagonal seams) until you have a continuous strip of bias binding that is the required length.

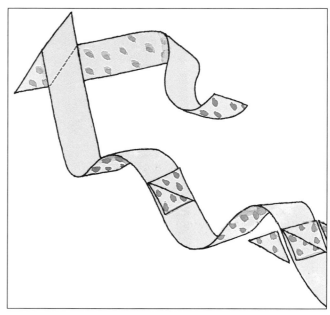

4 Fold the raw edges in to meet at the centre, and press. (Or use a commercial tapemaker.)

5 To bind an edge, unfold one edge of the binding. With right sides together, pin the binding along the edge to be bound, with the creaseline of the binding along the seamline. Stitch in the crease, and trim off the excess fabric if necessary. Wrap the binding over to the opposite side and pin along the folded edge. Slipstitch in place along the previous stitching line.

Piping

1 For piping, first make the bias binding. Divide what width it needs to be by wrapping a piece of fabric around the piping cord (which comes in different thicknesses) and adding 3cm (1¼in) to the width that was needed to enclose the cord. Make the binding to this width (see above).

2 With wrong side together, wrap the binding around the piping cord. Put the piping or zip foot on the machine, and, with the raw edges even, pin and stitch next to the cord.

3 To attach piping, place it on the right side of one piece of fabric, along the seamline, so that the cord is facing inwards. Pin and stitch just inside the seamline, close to the cord. At corners, clip into the seam allowance of the piping. Place the other fabric piece on top, with right sides together and raw edges even. Stitch through all four layers along the seamline, very close to the piping cord.

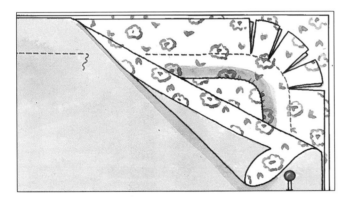

4 If you need to join the ends of the piping, position the join either centrally or at a seamline. Leave 1cm (³/₈in) unstitched at the first end and 5cm (2in) unstitched at the other end. Unpick the stitches of the binding at both ends, and fold the fabric back. Untwist the cord, trim the strands to varying lengths and then intertwine the strands from each end, overlapping the ends by about

2.5cm (1in). Fold the binding back in place, turn under the overlapping end of the binding and handsew.

Rouleaux

A rouleau is a narrow tube of fabric. Cut 2.5-3cm (1-1¼in) wide bias strips and join together (see Bias binding). Fold the strip in half lengthwise, right sides together, and raw edges even. Pin and stitch, taking a 6mm (¼in) seam allowance. Do not trim. To turn it right side out, sew the end onto a blunt-ended tapestry needle and push this through the tube. Remove the needle.

Hand stitches

Tacking (basting) is used to hold layers together temporarily. Fasten the end then take stitches about 1.3cm (½in) long. Remove the tacking when the machine stitching is complete.

Running stitch is used for gathering (and for hand stitching). Fasten the end then weave the needle in and out of the fabric, making small, evenly spaced stitches.

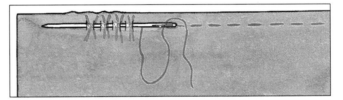

Slipstitch is used to sew a folded edge to a flat piece of fabric, or to sew two folded edges together. Work tiny stitches as shown so they are practically invisible.

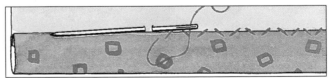

Herringbone stitch is used for handsewing curtain hems in place. Take small stitches first at the top (in the fold) then at the bottom (see page 42, step 10).

The Country House Style Living Room

COUNTRY HOUSE STYLE has a broad and enduring appeal that has made it probably the most dominant style of the twentieth century. With its use of rich, mellow surfaces, traditional designs and friendly clutter, it appeals to our need for comfort, security and cosiness.

To understand country house style, imagine a rather grand home that has been in the family for generations. Antique furniture and other high-quality furnishings have been collected over the years, and consequently reflect widely varying styles. This eclectic and sometimes slightly eccentric mix gives the home its unique charm and fascination. Similarly, the country house's blend of elegant furnishings and items reflecting country pursuits makes it unique and fascinating. Because the items have been passed down through the family, they have a well-used, much-loved look that tempers the grandeur.

The result is a look of faded glory and easy elegance which is not easy to imitate. The interior designer

Nancy Lancaster – who was the inspiration behind Colefax & Fowler, the influential fabric and design house that was largely responsible for the burgeoning popularity of this style in the twentieth century – used to leave expensive new sofas out in the rain so they would acquire the requisite worn-around-the-edges look. The practice of dipping new fabrics in tea or an onion-skin infusion has been another common ploy in the search for the antique look.

Soft furnishings play an important part in the country house look. Although chintz is most strongly associated with the style, this floral cotton has actually featured heavily in the country house drawing room only for the last few decades. Prior to that it was generally restricted to slip covers in the drawing room or dining room, and it only saw more general use in the bedroom.

Nevertheless, chintz has an illustrious history, having first become fashionable among the European aristocracy in the seventeenth century, when it was imported from India by the East India Companies. Hand-painted and hand-blocked, the fabric was known as "chints", which meant "speckled cloths". Initially it was only available in small pieces and so was used for table carpets, stool covers and similar purposes. Gradually, however, the size, colours and patterns of the Indian cloth were adapted to European requirements. Very soon, European workshops were copying the Indian fabrics, and by the late eighteenth century it was also being produced in America. The first half of the nineteenth century is regarded as the golden age of chintz, when wonderful prints were produced.

Today a wide variety of chintzes is available. Most chintzes, though not all, have a floral pattern printed in several colours on a light-coloured background. Many chintzes are glazed. Attractive as it looks, however, heavily glazed fabric is not particularly practical. The glaze, which gives a light sheen, makes the fabric less

flexible and will not withstand laundering. It may be better, therefore, to choose a chintz that is only lightly glazed or is completely unglazed.

Chintz can be used in profusion or with restraint, in combination with plain fabrics (or checks or stripes) or with other chintzes. Colefax & Fowler's dictum is that if you are using a chintz, you should use a lot of it – but use the same fabric throughout the room. This treatment works best if offset by large areas of plain colour. Another popular and fairly safe approach is to combine chintzes in related colourways but contrasting pattern scales.

However, one of the undeniable charms of the typical country house drawing room is its disregard for "rules" – a glorious jumble of colours and patterns blend happily together, their slightly faded tones softening any hard edges or colour clashes. The result is an overall harmony that looks, and is, completely unplanned.

Chintzes are most suitable for curtains, tablecloths, cushions and loose covers that will not get too much wear. They are not hard-wearing enough for upholstery.

Many other fabrics, some of which can be used for upholstery, as well as for other soft furnishings, have traditionally been used in the country house drawing room for much longer than chintz. These include wonderful damasks, brocades, woven tapestry fabrics, and silks (both plain and figured), as well as tartans and paisleys. Long before curtains were used at windows, the most luxurious of these fabrics adorned the walls of every self-respecting country house. When used for heavy, rather grand window treatments, complete with swags or pelmets (cornices), the more opulent fabrics look best in large rooms with well-proportioned windows. However, they can be used successfully in less grand rooms as cushions and as cloths for occasional tables. Other less sumptuous, plain, natural fabrics like cotton, linen or union can also work well.

PRECEDING SPREAD: Squashy sofas and armchairs, and an eclectic mix of high-quality textiles, characterize the country house look.

OPPOSITE: Eccentric combinations are not unusual in country house decor. This cosy alcove is separated from the rest of the room by paisley curtains. The draped curtains and exotic fringed pelmet are echoed by the fringed pelmet at the window, made from a tartan blanket, and the draped tartan curtains.

Window treatments in country house style rooms should incorporate generous amounts of fabric, and deep hems which drop right to the floor. Tiebacks and trimmings such as deep bullion fringes, braids, borders, ropes and tassels add to the overall look of quality and elegance.

Antique textiles – from rich tapestry weaves to exquisite laces and linens – provide an opportunity to add texture and instant antiquity to a room without having to inherit a family heirloom. Even relatively small pieces can be put to good use in cushion covers or as small cloths layered over others on side tables.

Today, the country house style is as relevant as ever, for its very timelessness is one of the reasons for its popularity. And the living room, with its cosy fireplace, variety of comfortable seating and collection of ornaments, offers perhaps the best example of this attractive and versatile style.

Rich fabrics, pleated curtains pooling onto the floor, and draped and tasselled swags and tails (cascades) provide a grand window treatment well suited to country house style.

Swathes of pleated and knotted silk provide an elegant frame to this window. The vibrant colour reappears in the cushion with a ruched gusset.

Bolster Cushion

Bolsters make very comfortable armrests. They look elegant on a daybed, chaise longue or plain divan.

1 Measure the circumference of the pad and add 3cm (1¼in). Measure the length and add 3cm (1¼in). Cut out one piece of fabric to these measurements.

2 Fold the fabric in half with right sides together; tack (baste) the long edges together. Stitch in from each side, leaving an opening as long as the zip. Press.

3 Place the zip right side down over the centre section of the seam; pin and tack in place. Turn the main section right side out. Stitch all around the zip. Remove the tacking stitches and partially open the zip.

4 Make up a length of covered piping cord, twice as long as the circumference of the pad, plus 4cm (1½in) for joins. Pin and tack covered piping around each end of the tube; join the ends to fit.

5 For the end sections cut two pieces of fabric the circumference of the bolster plus 3cm (1¼in) by the radius of one end plus 3cm (1¼in). Fold each piece in half with the right sides facing; pin and stitch the edges together, taking a 1.5cm (⅝in) seam allowance.

6 Turn in 1.5cm (⅝in) at one end of each end piece. Run two lines of hand gathering stitches around the folded edge.

7 Slide the end pieces over each end of the main section with right sides together. Pin and tack the raw edges of the end sections over the piping at each end of the main section. Stitch in place.

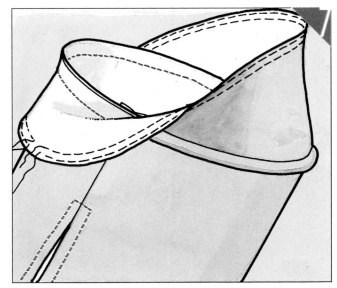

Materials Checklist
- ✿ Furnishing fabric
- ✿ Piping cord
- ✿ Matching sewing thread
- ✿ Two tassel ends with rosettes
- ✿ Bolster cushion pad
- ✿ Zip, 15cm (6in) shorter than bolster pad

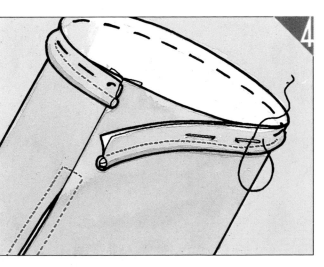

8 Insert the pad in the cover. Pull up the gathering threads at each end and fasten off. Sew the rosette ends of the tassels over each gathered end of the cover.

Curtain Valance

Chintz curtains surmounted by a matching valance are the epitome of country house style, though you could of course use a completely different fabric if you preferred. To make the curtains, follow the instructions for the Lined Triple-pleat Curtains on page 40.

1 Fix a valance shelf over the top of the curtains or a valance rail over the front of the curtain rail. If you will be hanging the valance from a shelf, you will need to use heading tape designed for use with touch-and-close tape. It is sewn onto the valance and stuck onto the shelf. Fix the tape along the front edge.

2 Measure the length of the valance shelf or rail including the returns (the sides of the shelf and rail). The side and centre lengths will need to be in proportion to the length of the curtains. Generally a valance should be one-sixth of the curtain length, plus 4cm (1½in) for hems and heading.

3 Mark out a paper pattern to this size. Mark in the returns on either side, then the centre. Measure the chosen length at the sides and in the centre and draw a curved line to join the two together. Fold the paper vertically along the centre line and cut along the shaped hem edge. Unfold and check the shape at the window.

4 Cut out sheets of paper to the chosen outside length by twice the width of the valance pattern. Mark the outside return marks. Divide the original pattern, between returns, vertically into 20cm (8in) sections.

5 Cut up each vertical line and, using masking tape, fix in place on the new pattern sheet, spreading the original pattern apart, between the outside return marks, at each vertical division. Even out the pattern so the excess is spread equally across the whole pattern. Then fold the pattern in half along the centre mark and cut along the shaped base line.

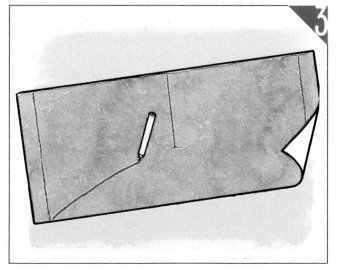

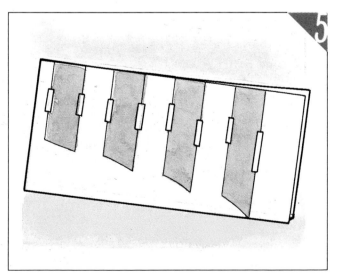

6 Cut out as many fabric widths to the correct length as you need to make up the overall length. Pin and stitch the fabric widths together with plain seams, matching any pattern across each seam. Press the seams open. Repeat, to make up a piece of lining in the same way.

7 Place the fabric and lining with right sides together. Pin the pattern centrally to the fabrics, matching centres. Cut out both layers, adding a 1.5cm (5⁄8in) seam allowance all around.

8 Remove the pattern. Pin and stitch the side and base edges together. Trim and turn right side out. Press. Trim 1.5cm (5⁄8in) off the top edge of the lining. Tack (baste) the lining to the fabric across the top edge. Turn 1.5cm (5⁄8in) of fabric over the top edge of the lining and tack across the valance.

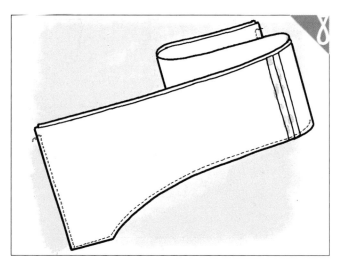

9 Position the heading tape on the wrong side of the valance, placing the top edge just down from the top folded edge of the valance. At one end, pull out heading tape cords, and knot. Turn under 1.5cm (5⁄8in) of heading tape; pin.

10 At the opposite end, pull out the heading tape cords from the front of the tape and leave them hanging free. Turn under the tape end for 1.5cm (5⁄8in). Tack, then stitch the tape into position all around, catching down the knotted tapes, but leaving the cords free at the opposite end.

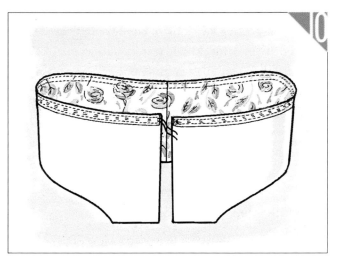

11 Position the fringe on the right side of the valance, so the fringe edge matches the base edge of the valance. Tuck under the fringe ends to fit; pin and stitch the fringe in place.

12 Pull up the heading tape from the free cord end, until it fits the shelf or rail, and knot the cords together to hold. Wind up excess cord neatly and hold at one side with a few handstitches.

13 Lay the cord across the valance centrally over the heading tape, and tie the ends into a decorative knot at each side. Handsew in position over the gathers, pushing the ends in between the lining and fabric at each side. Hang the valance in place, either by pressing touch-and-close sections together or with curtain hooks onto a rail.

Braid-trimmed Cushions

Cushions covered in sumptuous brocade and rich braid trimmings will give a look of comfort and grandeur. Combine them with antique textiles and woven tapestry fabrics for an even more opulent look.

Gold cushion

Finished size: 40cm (16in) square

1 Positioning the fabric pattern centrally, cut one 43cm (17¼in) square for cushion front and two pieces each 43x23cm (17¼x9¼in) for cushion backs.

2 Place the back sections with right sides together; pin and tack (baste) one long edge along the seamline, taking a 1.5cm (⅝in) seam allowance. Stitch each end of the tacked seam for 6.5cm (2⅝in) leaving 30cm (12in) unstitched (in other words, only tacked) in the centre. Press seam open.

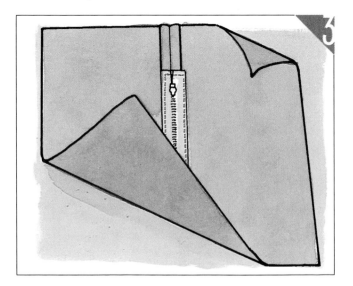

3 Place the zip right side down over the tacked section of the seam. Pin and tack in place. Working from the right side, stitch in place all around the zip. Remove the tacking stitches.

4 Partially open the zip. Place back to front with right sides together; pin and stitch all around the cushion cover. Trim and neaten the seams. Open the zip and turn right side out.

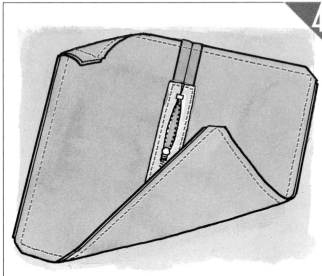

5 Tack fringing around the outer edge of the cushion, joining the ends together to fit and mitring the corners. Position braid around the outer edge of the cushion, covering the top of the fringing and mitring the corners in the same way. Pin and handsew in place, down both edges of braid, catching in the edge of the fringing at the same time. Insert the cushion pad through the zip opening.

Materials Checklist

- ✿ 50cm (½yd) of 122cm (48in) wide gold brocade fabric
- ✿ 1.80m (2yd) of 1.5cm (⅝in) wide braid
- ✿ 1.80m (2yd) of 4.5cm (1⅝in) wide fringing
- ✿ 30cm (12in) zip
- ✿ 40cm (16in) square cushion pad
- ✿ Matching sewing thread

Red and gold cushion

Finished size: 40cm (16in) square

1 Positioning the fabric design centrally, cut one 43cm (17¼in) square of fabric for the front. Cut two pieces each 43x23cm (17¼x9¼in) for the cushion back.

2 Insert the zip into the cushion back in the same way as for the gold cushion, steps 2-4.

3 Lay out the cushion front with the right side uppermost. Position petersham ribbon around the cushion front with the outer edge 1.5cm (⅝in) from the outer edge of the cushion. Mitre the ribbon at each corner and position the ends together under one mitre. Pin and tack in place. Pin and tack braid over the outer edge of the petersham ribbon, mitring the corners in the same way. Topstitch the inner edge of the petersham ribbon, leaving a small gap at one corner. Topstitch along both edges of the braid.

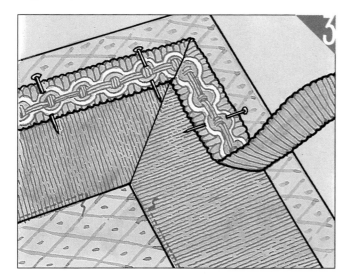

4 Place cushion front to back with right sides together. Pin and stitch together all around, alongside the braid edge, taking a 1.5cm (⅝in) seam allowance. Trim and neaten the seam. Turn the cover right side out.

5 Handsew cord around the inner edge of the petersham ribbon, pushing the ends into the gap in the ribbon at one corner.

6 Cut eight tassels from braid and handsew two tassels into each corner with the heads against the cord and the tassels facing out towards the corners. Insert the cushion pad through the zip opening.

Green and blue cushion

Finished size: 40cm (16in) square

1 Make this cushion in the same way as the red and gold cushion, steps 1-5, substituting tassel braid for the plain braid in step 3.

2 Cut four tassels from the remaining braid and handsew into each corner with each head against the cord and the tassel facing towards the corner. Insert the cushion pad through the zip opening.

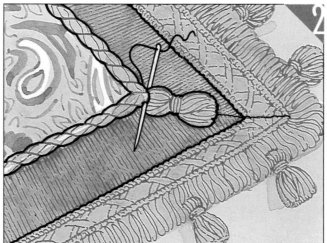

Materials Checklist

- ✿ 50cm (½yd) of 122cm (48in) wide red-and-gold brocade fabric
- ✿ 1.80m (2yd) of 5cm (2in) wide petersham ribbon
- ✿ 1.80m (2yd) of 2cm (¾in) wide braid
- ✿ 1.40m (1½yd) of thick cord
- ✿ 12cm (5in) length of tassel braid – enough for eight tassels
- ✿ 30cm (12in) zip
- ✿ 40cm (16in) square cushion pad
- ✿ Matching sewing thread

Materials Checklist

- ✿ 50cm (½yd) of 122cm (48in) wide multi-coloured brocade
- ✿ 2m (2¼yd) of 6cm (2¼in) wide tassel braid
- ✿ 1.80m (2yd) of 5cm (2in) wide petersham ribbon
- ✿ 1.40m (1½yd) of plain cord
- ✿ 30cm (12in) zip
- ✿ 40cm (16in) square cushion pad
- ✿ Matching sewing threads

Display Tablecloths

Cloths on an occasional table can be used to emphasize the style and colour scheme of a room. For a country house style drawing room, chintz or damask would be particularly appropriate. As the cloth goes all the way to the floor, what is underneath doesn't matter – it could be an inexpensive chipboard (particle board) table or even a filing cabinet with a chipboard circle on top.

Circular damask cloth

Finished size: 190cm (75in) in diameter

1 Cut two 193cm (76in) lengths, matching the pattern repeat. With right sides together, pin and stitch the two lengths together down one long edge. Press the seam.

2 To make a pattern on a 100cm (39½in) square of newspaper or brown paper, tie a pencil to a piece of string 96.5cm (38in) long (allowing extra for tying). Hold the end of the string at one corner and draw an arc.

3 Fold the fabric along the seamline, then fold that in half. Using the quarter-circle pattern, cut out a circle from the damask.

4 If you are not trimming the edge, zigzag stitch around the raw edge of the circle, then press under 1cm (³⁄₈in) all around. Pin and stitch.

5 If you *are* trimming the edge, turn 1cm (³⁄₈in) to the right side all around the edge. Pin and stitch. Pin braid on top, covering the raw edge. Stitch, turning under the ends of the braid.

Square toile de Jouy & chintz cloths

Finished size: *toile de Jouy* 114cm (45in) square; chintz 80cm (31½in) square

1 If you are not trimming the edges, turn under a 1cm (³⁄₈in) double hem on each edge. Press, pin and stitch.

2 If you *are* trimming the edges, turn 1cm (³⁄₈in) to the right side; press and stitch. Stitch braid on top.

Broderie anglaise (eyelet) square

Finished size: 32cm (12½in) square

1 With right sides together, pin the edging along one edge of the square. Stitch, taking a 1cm (³⁄₈in) seam allowance, stopping 1cm (³⁄₈in) short of each edge.

2 Repeat for the other three edges, then mitre the corners neatly.

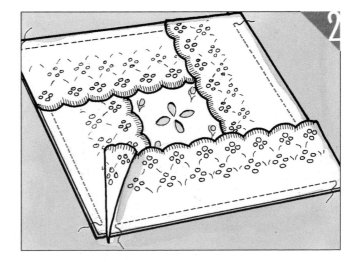

Materials Checklist

✿ 3.90m (4¼yd) of 122cm (48in) or 136cm (54in) wide damask fabric (plus one extra pattern repeat for matching)
✿ 1.20m (1⅓yd) of toile de Jouy fabric 122cm (48in) wide
✿ 90cm (1yd) of 90cm (36in) or 122cm (48in) wide chintz fabric
✿ Braid or fringe (optional): 6m (6.6yd) for damask; 4.6m (5yd) for toile de Jouy; 3.2m (3½yd) for chintz
✿ 21cm (8¼in) square broderie anglaise (eyelet) fabric plus 1.40m (1½yd) of 7.5cm (3in) wide broderie anglaise (eyelet) edging
✿ Matching sewing threads

Pleated Lampshade

A pleated fabric lampshade looks sophisticated yet cosy. Its classic styling makes it suitable for a variety of lamp bases. Choose a cream colour for maximum light, or a warm tone for atmosphere.

1 Bind around the top ring with tape. Begin at one strut and wind the tape over the ring at an angle, covering the top end to hold it. At the end, knot the tape in a figure of eight at the first strut position.

2 Measure the height of the lampshade frame and add an extra 10cm (4in). Measure around the base ring. Add one-quarter of this measurement to the base measurement for fullness. Cut a rectangle of fabric to these measurements. You may have to join two pieces of fabric to gain the width; if so, cut two pieces to the same length, so the seams will be equally placed.

3 Join the fabric pieces together into a ring. Pin and stitch together with narrow flat-fell seams.

4 Turn under the lower edge to form a double 1cm (³⁄₈in) wide casing; pin and stitch around the casing leaving a small gap over one of the seams.

5 Fasten one end of the fine cord into a bodkin. Run the bodkin around the casing, leaving two long ends free at the gap. Fit the cover over the frame and pin the top to the bound top ring to hold temporarily. Pull up the cord around the lower edge, so the fabric gathers up into small pleats. Space out the gathers evenly around the shade and check that the overlap is the same width all around; tie cord ends together and cut off the ends.

6 With the fabric grain running up the shade, pin the fabric to the tape on either side and at the top and base of the top ring, so there is an equal amount of fabric between each pin.

7 Work around the lampshade top, pleating up the excess fabric between each set of pins. Make sure that the pleats are equal and even. Continue pleating around the shade.

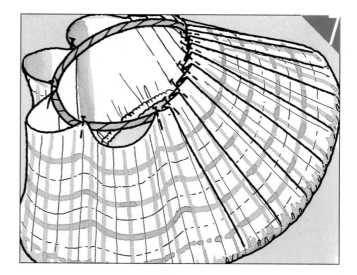

8 Check the pleating to make sure it looks even. Then, using a double sewing thread, oversew the pleats in place to the tape on the right side of the frame. Make sure that the stitches are small and firm. When the stitching is complete, carefully snip off the excess fabric just above the stitching line.

9 Use fabric adhesive to stick ribbon around the base and top edges. Turn under the ribbon ends and butt join over one of the seams.

Materials Checklist

✪ Sloping lampshade frame
✪ 70cm (³⁄₄yd) of 90cm (36in) wide fine cotton or lightweight silk fabric
✪ Matching sewing thread
✪ 6mm (¹⁄₄in) wide white tape
✪ 150cm (60in) of white cord
✪ Bodkin
✪ 2m (2¹⁄₈yd) of 6mm (¹⁄₄in) wide embossed ribbon
✪ Fabric adhesive

The Neoclassical Style Dining Room

NEOCLASSICAL STYLE actually covers a very broad area historically. All Neoclassicism is derived from the Classicism of ancient Greece and Rome but has been interpreted in various ways over the centuries. The Renaissance, in the fifteenth and sixteenth centuries, represented a rebirth of ancient Classical ideals, especially Roman. Inspiration was drawn from the Classical civilizations, and architecture and interiors began to feature decorative motifs from Roman architecture and sculpture.

Then, in the early eighteenth century in Britain, and fifty years later in America, the so-called Palladian revival brought a return to Classical ideas, in reaction to the ornate Baroque style that had dominated the previous century.

*PRECEDING SPREAD:
Frivolous chair
covers and graceful
swags soften the
formality of this
dining room.*

*RIGHT: Black and
white fabric
printed with crisp,
highly detailed
classical subjects or
architectural
images looks
dramatic in any
Neoclassical
scheme.*

However, the late eighteenth century is the period most associated with Neoclassicism throughout Europe and America. It developed as a reaction to the frivolous, curvaceous Rococo style, as a result of the discovery of the buried Roman cities of Pompeii and Herculaneum. This style persisted into the early nineteenth century, in the form of Regency (Britain), Empire (France), Federal (America), and Biedermeier (Germany).

Thus, Neoclassicism can include a multitude of styles, but all of them originate in Classical Greece and Rome (and, to a lesser extent, ancient Egypt).

Classical/Neoclassical motifs include "grotesques", a type of ornamentation incorporating human and animal figures combined with flowers and foliage symmetrically intertwined. (The name comes from the Roman ornament found in underground chambers known as grottoes.) Other motifs include swags and garlands, cornucopias, urns, lion masks, cherubs, entwining scrolls, the Greek key, acanthus and anthemion (honeysuckle). Symmetry, harmony, balance and proportion are the keynotes of the style.

Adam, Hepplewhite and Sheraton are all names associated with Neoclassical interiors and furniture of the late eighteenth century. Fashions of the time included *trompe l'oeil*, which literally means "deceiving the eye" and involves the use of perspective and shading to paint realistic-looking scenes; examples include murals and *trompe l'oeil* balustrades and columns. Other paint effects such as marbling

and graining (to make a surface look like marble or expensive wood) were also fashionable, as were wallpapers simulating marble or stucco, or depicting architectural features or Classical motifs. Print rooms, in which monochrome engravings were pasted on the walls along with paper bows, cords, frames, etc, appeared at this time too.

Toile de Jouy *fabric, which first appeared in the Neoclassical period of the late eighteenth century, featured finely etched pictorial scenes.*

Colour schemes often imitated the colours the Romans were believed to have used. Particularly popular was a terracotta shade inspired by the reds on antique Greek vases.

Curtains and drapery were used to soften the severe Classical architecture, with opulent fabrics and styles. Initially, pull-up curtains were hung at the windows. These were the forerunners of today's Austrian and festoon blinds but were simpler; when pulled down, they hung flat against the window, with no gathering. Later, they became fuller and were usually topped with carved wooden cornices.

Conventional draw curtains were also introduced as were muslin subcurtains. Another fashion was "reefed", or "Italian-strung", curtains, which pulled up and apart by means of diagonally strung cords, rather like theatre curtains. Swags and other drapery were particularly fashionable in the Neoclassical period.

Silk damasks and brocades were widely used, and the *toile de Jouy* also appeared at this time. This cotton fabric printed with Neoclassical designs (such as mythological subjects, contemporary events, rustic scenes or Classical architecture) in a single colour, usually on an off-white background, is enjoying renewed popularity today. It was originally copperplate-printed, with the soft toile effect created by repeatedly washing and bleaching the fabric and then passing it through rollers. Although toiles were first printed in Ireland, they take their name from the famous factory at Jouy-en-Josas, France, which produced them from 1770 onwards.

Classicism had began to appear in homes other than just those of the aristocracy by the early nineteenth century. By this time, ancient Egypt had become another source of inspiration, and Napoleon's Egyptian campaign resulted in a fashion for military-style furnishings such as tented walls and ceilings (in very unmilitary brocades, silks and chintzes) and the Trafalgar chair (which had sabre legs).

Cloud-effect ceilings were popular, as were "scenic" wallpapers, which provided a mural-effect panorama around a room. Red was a popular colour for dining rooms.

The early nineteenth century was the golden age of window treatments, which were the focal point of rooms. An elegant layered look was typical of this period, with blinds, silk or muslin undercurtains and outer curtains. They hung from a decorative, often gilded pole with Classical ornament such as laurel wreaths, eagles or rosettes. The pole might be suspended from a cornice or be draped with swags, and the full-length curtains were caught back with tiebacks or holdbacks when open.

Trimmings such as deep heavy fringing, rich braids, ornate tassels, rosettes and embroidered borders were very important at this time. Towards the end of the period, continuous drapery was used to link two or more windows on a wall.

Fabrics used in Neoclassical interiors of the late eighteenth and early nineteenth centuries included damasks, brocatelles, taffetas and velvets as well as the lighter silks and muslins. Rich shades of blue, turquoise, raspberry, cherry, violet and saffron yellow were popular.

Neoclassical interiors have become popular again in the closing years of the twentieth century, but today they are often designed with a lighter touch and even a sense of humour. Fabrics printed with "architectural" motifs in crisp black and white are one way of introducing a Neoclassical flavour with a distinctly upbeat, modern feel. The whole room (or entire home) can follow the theme, or just a few Neoclassical elements may be included.

If you decide to use the style in just one room, the dining room is particularly suitable, as the window(s), dining table and chairs all provide an excellent opportunity to bring in a variety of Neoclassical designs and fabrics.

OPPOSITE: *Neoclassicism with a modern twist. Tented walls and ceiling, and ropes and tassels, all of which featured heavily in Regency and Empire rooms, are here used in a witty 1990s way.*

Lined Triple-pleat Curtains

Classic lined, triple-pleat silk curtains are given the grand treatment by draping them back with gold cord and tassels. Although this type of curtain may incorporate hand-sewn pleats, a heading tape will also give an elegant, tailored look.

1 Measure the length of the track each curtain will hang from, add 10cm (4in) for the side hems and then multiply this figure by 2.

2 Divide the width of the fabric into the curtain measurement to find the number of widths you'll need for each curtain. If the figure is over halfway between two widths, round the number of widths up to the next full width. If the figure is under halfway, add only an extra half width. Always place any half widths on the outside edge of a curtain, where they will be less obvious than near the centre.

Materials Checklist

❋ *Furnishing fabric*
❋ *Lining fabric*
❋ *Triple-pleat curtain heading tape and hooks*
❋ *Matching sewing thread*
❋ *Lead curtain weights (optional)*
❋ *Cord tidies (optional)*
❋ *Tieback cords and tassels (optional)*

3 To find how much fabric you'll need, measure from the curtain track to the desired length and add the depth of the curtain heading tape, plus 10cm (4in) for the hem. Multiply this measurement by the number of curtain widths to find the total amount of fabric you need. Finally, if the fabric has a prominent pattern repeat allow one extra pattern repeat per fabric width, after the first width.

4 When cutting out each length, either pull out a thread across the fabric first, to use as a cutting guide; or cut out following the pattern. On patterned fabric, position any main pattern motifs on the hem edge, as incomplete motifs are less obvious in the gathered heading. Mark across the fabric on the wrong side along the base of the motifs; measure the hem allowance below this line and cut across the fabric. Then measure up from the cut edge to the correct length for the curtain and cut across the fabric.

5 Using the first length as a template, cut out all the fabric widths for the curtain. To do this, lay the first length alongside the uncut fabric. Match the pattern across the side edges and cut the next length, trimming off any excess fabric at either end. Repeat to cut out all the lengths.

6 To cut the lining, as there is no pattern, after straightening the fabric edge simply measure and cut each length.

7 For each curtain pin the fabric widths together, being careful to match any pattern across the seamlines and across each pair of curtains. Stitch each seam, taking a 1.5cm (⅝in) seam allowance. Press the seams open. Clip into the selvedge edge at regular intervals to prevent puckering.

8 Stitch the lining widths together in the same way, but do not snip into the seam allowances of the lining. Press the seams open.

9 Lay the curtain flat, wrong side up. Turn in and press a 5cm (2in) hem down both side edges. Turn up and press a 10cm (4in) hem along the base edges. Use pins to mark at the base edge where the side hem edge falls, and to mark at the side edge where the base edge falls.

10 Unfold the hems and turn in the corner from pin to pin. Refold the hems over the turned-in corners. If desired, sew lead curtain weights into the corners to help the curtain hang better. Herringbone stitch the hems in place along the side and base edges.

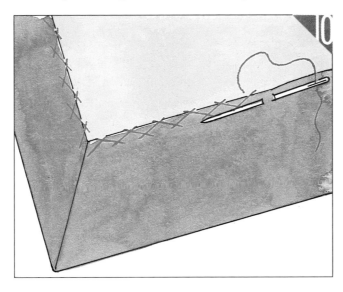

11 Lay the curtain flat, wrong side up. With wrong sides together, centre the lining on top, matching the top edges. Pin together down the centre. Turn back the lining to one side over the pins. Lockstitch both fabrics together to just above the hem edge.

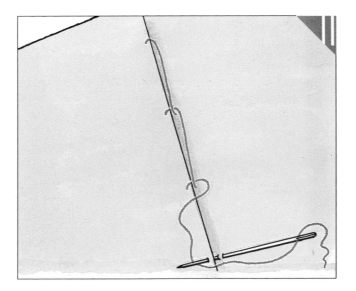

12 Turn back the lining over the curtain and pin together again on either side of the centre at approximately 40cm (16in) intervals. Turn back the curtain at each position and lockstitch the two fabrics together as before. Repeat as necessary across the width of the curtain.

13 Trim off excess lining so the raw side and base edges of the lining match the hemmed side and base edges of the curtain. Now turn under the lining for 2.5cm (1in) down the side edges and pin. Turn up a 5cm (2in) hem on the base edge of the lining, forming neat base corners, and pin. Slipstitch the lining to the curtain along the side and base edges of the curtain.

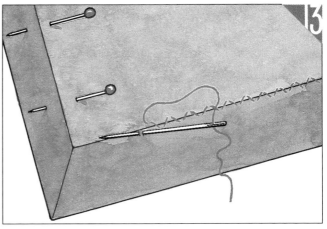

14 Turn down the top edge of the curtain fabric and lining to the same width as the heading and press. Unfold and trim off the lining to the pressed line. Turn down the curtain fabric again; pin and tack (baste).

15 Position the curtain heading tape on the wrong side of the curtain with the top edge just down from the folded edge of the curtain. Check that the triple pleats will match across adjoining curtains. (In other words, the distance from the last pleat on one curtain to the first one on the adjacent curtain should be the same as the distance between other pleats.)

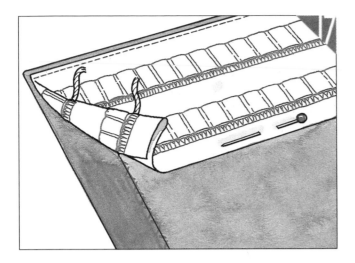

16 At the centre edge of the curtain pull out the cords on the wrong side of the tape and knot. Turn under the tape edge in line with the curtain edge and trim down to 2cm ($^3/4$in). At the outside edge, pull the cords out from the right side of the tape and leave them hanging free. Turn under the tape end as before.

17 Pin, tack and stitch the heading tape in place along both edges, stitching both rows in the same direction. Catch down the cords at the leading edge (ie the edge that will be in the centre) but leave the cords hanging free at the outside edge.

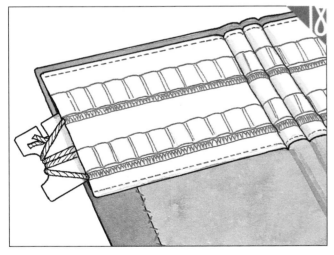

18 Holding the cords together, pull up fully from the outside edge to form the pleats, then ease out until the curtain measures the correct width. Knot the cords together, but do not cut off the excess, as they will need to be unpleated for cleaning. If desired, wind the excess cords around a cord tidy and fit it into the heading tape at the outside edge.

19 Slot a hook through the heading tape behind each pleat and at each end. (Whether you use the top or bottom row of pockets depends on whether the track is to be seen or not.) Hang the curtains, and arrange them, open, into even pleats. Tie two or three scarves or strips of spare fabric around them, and leave overnight to "train" the pleats to hold their shape.

20 If desired, close the curtains and drape them back using cord tiebacks with tassels.

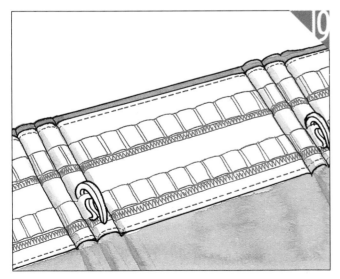

Chair Covers

Slip covers have for centuries been used to protect fine upholstery. But if an attractive fabric and stylish design are used, they can look as good as the upholstery they are protecting – and, of course, they have the advantage of being removable for cleaning. The ties on the backs of these covers, though not functional, add a whimsical touch.

Measuring the chair

1 Measure the seat from the back edge over the front and down to the seat edge. Measure across the seat from side edge to side edge. Cut out one square of fabric to this size, adding 2cm (3/4in) all around.

2 For the inside back, measure the length from the top back edge to the seat. Measure the width from the back side edge around to the other back side edge. Cut a piece of fabric to this size, adding 2cm (3/4in) all around for seams.

3 For the outside back, measure from the top of the back to the back seat edge. Measure across the back width. Cut one piece of fabric to this size, adding 2cm (3/4in) all around for seams.

4 For the skirt, measure all around the seat where the skirt top will be and add 34cm (13½in) for each front and back pleat. Measure the length from the seat to the floor and add 4.5cm (1¾in) for the seam and hem. Cut out one piece of fabric to these measurements. If necessary, pin and stitch fabric widths together to gain the correct width.

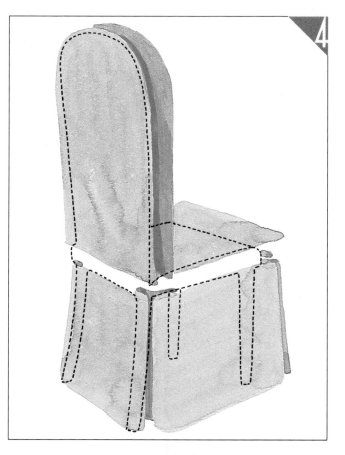

5 Lay the inside back piece on the chair, wrong side up, and either hand gather the fabric around each outside edge and pull up the gathers evenly; or alternatively, make small darts at the sides of the top in order to ease in the fullness. Fasten off.

6 Make up sufficient covered piping cord (see page 14) from the chair cover fabric to fit around the outside back and around the top of the skirt. Pin and tack (baste) the piping around the outside back piece, matching the raw edges.

Materials Checklist
- ✪ *Furnishing fabric*
- ✪ *Piping cord*
- ✪ *Matching sewing thread*

7 Pin the inside back to the outside back, catching in the piping cord. Slip it over the chair back and adjust the pins if necessary. Adjust the tacked piping too if necessary. Remove from the chair, and stitch. Trim the seams, snipping into the curves.

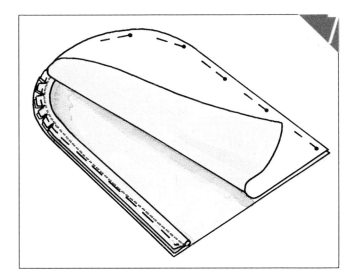

8 Lay the seat cover over the chair seat, wrong side up. Pin the excess fabric at each front corner into a pleat and catch together. Pin the seat to the inside back. Remove from the chair and stitch, continuing the stitching to the outside back down to the skirt edge. Trim and neaten the seams.

9 Pin and stitch the covered piping around the skirt edge of the cover, joining the ends together to fit. Pin and stitch the skirt into a ring; neaten and press the seam open. Neaten the hem edge of the skirt. Turn up the hem edge for 2.5cm (1in); pin and stitch. Mark the centre of each pleat. Fold in an 8.5cm (3¼in) wide pleat over the centre marks; tack across top edge.

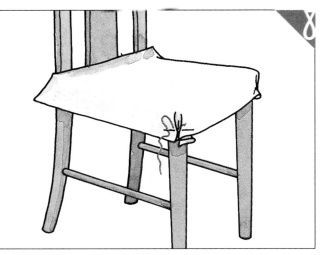

10 Place the cover over the chair once more, and pin the skirt to the lower edge of the cover over the piping. Remove from the chair, and stitch. Neaten the seams and turn the cover right side out.

11 For each tie cut a strip of fabric 114x18cm (45x7in). Fold each strip in half; pin and stitch the long and short edges, leaving an opening. Trim and turn right side out. Turn in the opening edges and slipstitch.

12 Position the centre of each tie over the back pleat; pin and topstitch in place with a rectangle of stitching. Tie the ends together into a bow.

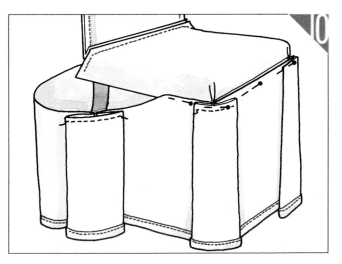

Curtains with Ties

Many of the elements of this dining room are Neo-classical yet the overall impression is lighthearted and frivolous. The scallop-edged curtains in particular contribute to this effect.

An unusual feature of these curtains is the delightful scalloped edge in a contrasting fabric. However, what makes the curtains really unusual is their ties. Although they appear to hold the curtains on the pole, in fact the curtains are supported by rings behind the bows. This allows them to be opened and closed easily, which would be awkward if the ties were the means of support. The instructions for making them are given below.

The simple slip-on chair covers in the photograph are made in much the same way as the covers on page 44, but with only a short, unpleated skirt. The seat cover is cut to the shape of the seat, with piping around the front and sides. The short front skirt has a scalloped lower edge, and the outside back has a scalloped lower edge to match the front. The inside back has two small darts at each top corner, rather than gathers, and is piped all around. The covers are stitched together in the same way as the chair covers with the long skirts.

1 For each curtain, measure across the curtain pole, and double that measurement. Measure from the pole to the floor and add 3cm (1¼in) for hem and heading. Cut out as many fabric widths as necessary to gain the correct width.

2 Pin and stitch the curtain widths together with plain seams. Clip into the seam allowances on the selvedge edges to prevent puckering, and press open. Repeat to make up the lining to match.

3 Make a paper pattern for the scallop edging. Cut a 20cm (8in) wide strip of paper the same length as the curtain. Fold the paper up into equal lengths, approximately 15cm (6in) long. Use a pair of compasses or a small plate, and mark a semi-circle on one long edge to form a curve. Keeping the paper folded, cut around the curved edge. Unfold the pattern.

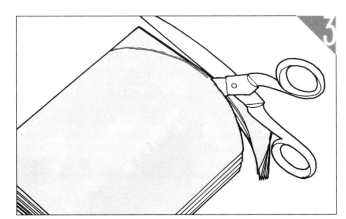

4 Use the pattern to cut two scalloped strips of contrasting fabric for each curtain, adding 1.5cm (⅝in) all around for seams. Place the strips with right sides together; pin and stitch all around the scallops. Trim and turn right side out. Pin and tack (baste) the long raw edges together.

5 Position the scalloped edges on the right side of each curtain down the leading edge (the edge you would pull to close the curtain), beginning and ending 1.5cm (⅝in) from the bottom and top edges. Place the lining on the fabric with right sides together. Pin and stitch together along the side and base edges, catching in the edgings. Trim and turn right side out.

Materials Checklist

- ✿ *Furnishing fabric*
- ✿ *Contrasting fabric for edging*
- ✿ *Contrasting fabric for ties*
- ✿ *Lining fabric*
- ✿ *Triple-pleat curtain heading tape and hooks*
- ✿ *Curtain rings*
- ✿ *2 cord tidies (optional)*
- ✿ *Matching sewing thread*
- ✿ *Lead curtain weights (optional)*
- ✿ *Paper for pattern*

6 For each curtain tie, cut a strip of contrasting fabric 33x7cm (13x2¾in). Fold it in half lengthwise with right sides together; pin and stitch the long edge and one short edge, taking a 1.5cm (⅝in) seam allowance. Trim and turn right side out.

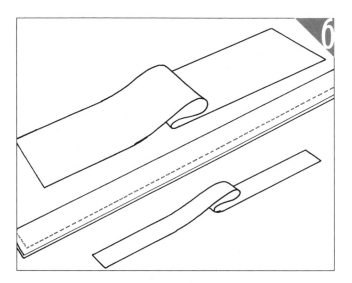

7 Turn the top edge of the curtain fabric and lining down together for 1.5cm (⅝in). Position the heading tape along the top edge on the wrong side. At each point where there will be a pleat, position a pair of ties, one on top of the other, tucking the raw ends under the heading tape. Pin the heading tape on the top edge in the same way as for Lined Triple-pleat Curtains (see page 43), covering the ends of the ties. Stitch in place.

8 Pull up the tape to form pleats (see page 43) and fix a hook behind each pleat. If desired, wind the excess cord around a cord tidy.

9 Hang the curtains from curtain rings on the curtain pole. Knot the ties together and into bows around the base of each curtain ring.

Gusseted Seat Cushion

Comfortable yet with tailored, classic lines, a cushion with a gusset is ideal for use on a dining chair. By cutting the fabric and foam to the exact shape of the chair seat, you can make a firm cushion with an almost upholstered look. For a Neoclassical decor, choose a Regency stripe, an "architectural" print or a *toile de Jouy* fabric.

1 To make the cushion pattern, place the paper over the chair seat. Holding the paper firmly in place, mark around the outer edge with a pencil. Remove the paper and fold it in half from front to back. Cut out the shape following the marked outline. Replace the pattern on the chair seat and check for fit. Mark in the positions of the back ties.

2 Place the pattern on the foam and mark around it with a felt tip pen. Cut out the foam shape, using an electric carving knife or serrated bread knife.

3 Use the pattern to cut two pieces from fabric, adding a 1.5cm (5⁄8in) seam allowance all around. For the gusset, measure around the outer edge of the pattern and cut out 8cm (3¼in) wide strips to this length plus 3cm (1¼in). You may have to join two pieces to gain the correct length; if so, position two seams in the same place on either side of the cushion.

4 Pin and tack (baste) cord around the cushion top with the cord facing inwards, and joining the ends together neatly in the centre of the back edge to fit. Repeat, to stitch cord around the cushion base in the same way. Clip into the seam allowance at the corners.

5 Cut the ribbon into four equal lengths. Pin a length of ribbon at each tie position on either side of the back cushion piece, pinning each so that it is parallel to the side edges.

6 Pin and stitch the gusset into a ring. Place the gusset on the cushion top with right sides together, raw edges even. Pin and stitch the gusset to the cushion top, catching in the cord.

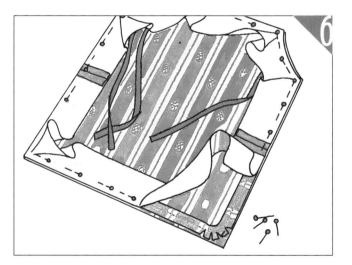

7 Repeat, to stitch the opposite edge of the gusset to the cushion base, catching in the cord and ties and leaving an opening across the centre back. Trim the seams, snipping into the curves and corners. Turn the cushion right side out.

8 Insert the foam. Turn in the opening edges and slipstitch together to close. Place the cushion on the chair seat, fasten the ties around the back struts of the chair and tie into bows.

Materials Checklist

✿ 70cm (3⁄4yd) of 122cm (48in) wide Regency stripe fabric
✿ 50cm (20in) square of 5cm (2in) thick foam
✿ 2.50m (2³⁄4yd) of inserting cord trim
✿ Matching sewing thread
✿ Paper for pattern
✿ 1.30m (1¹⁄2yd) of 13mm (1⁄2in) wide ribbon for ties

The Gustavian Style Hall

Gustavian style is the name given to Sweden's unique version of Neoclassicism, which developed in the late eighteenth century during the reign of Gustav III. As elsewhere, it represented a reaction to the Rococo style that had prevailed earlier in the century, and it was characterized by symmetry, straight lines, and restraint. However, the Gustavian look is very distinctive and different from the Neoclassicism found elsewhere in Europe. Cool and elegant, it is simultaneously simple and sophisticated, and it encompasses an attractive blend of Neoclassical restraint and rococo frivolity.

Motifs such as laurel wreaths, garlands, rosettes, medallions and urns, which were very much a feature of Gustavian interiors, are completely classical in origin. Yet they were combined with light, delicate, curvilinear rococo motifs and ornamentation, which offset any classical severity. (During the late Gustavian period, however, the rococo element disappeared, and the style became more heavily Neoclassical.)

The most distinctive feature of Gustavian rooms was the wonderful wall decoration. Classical motifs such as laurel swags and Greek key borders were combined with rococo designs of birds and butterflies, twining flowers and posies. The decorations were painted onto stretched canvas panels fixed to the walls above the painted wainscoting. Sometimes family portrait medallions were hung in the centre of the panels, surrounded by classical ornament, marbling or painted borders.

Even more recognizably Gustavian were the tall, columnar, ceramic-tiled stoves, used for heating the houses. Other typical features of the Gustavian interior include the use of chalky pastel paintwork on furniture, with the woodgrain showing through slightly. Gustavian colours are subtle greys (including blue-greys, grey-greens and pearl-greys) and straw yellow, highlighted with a discreet hint of gold leaf. Chairs were often painted in one of the colours used in the decor, especially the colour of the panelling behind it. Sparkling crystal in the form of chandeliers or wall sconces was popular, and gilt mirrors with a distinctive ribbon top-knot were also very fashionable.

It's not necessary to have painted wall panels and a tiled stove to give a room a Gustavian flavour. Here the colour scheme, simple furniture and gingham curtains create the fresh, cool, airy feeling found in a Gustavian interior.

Walls or painted panelling up to dado (chair) rail or picture (plate) rail height, in the same pale, chalky colours, and bleached, almost-white floorboards are also very Gustavian.

Curtains too should be cool and simple; muslin or checked gingham have exactly the right feel, as do lengths of filmy lace. The painted wooden furniture was often given little square cushions, in plain or checked fabrics.

The quality of light in Gustavian rooms is very distinctive. Like most northern countries, where winter nights are long and light is at a premium, Swedish rooms were designed to allow in and reflect the maximum amount of light. Thus, as well as pale, faded-looking walls, bleached floorboards and white plastered

Scarf drapery provides an attractive alternative to muslin or gingham curtains for a window in a Gustavian style room. Here, a large cutwork stole and a small lace-edged cloth are draped elegantly over a pole.

ceilings, and the use of mirrors, chandeliers and candle sconces, the Gustavian home had tall windows. These were given thin white cotton curtains, which in the grander homes were surmounted by festoons and swags usually in the same fabric. Often muslin swags were used without any curtains at all. To protect the furnishings inside the room from sunlight, roller blinds were also used.

If you like the elegance and simplicity of Gustavian style but do not want elaborate swags and festoons at your windows, simpler treatments are also suitable. Muslin curtains with a fixed (stationary) heading, held back by a table which they gracefully frame, are very much in keeping. So are windows dressed with nothing but very deep muslin valances. Rather than conventional pinch pleats, the valances can have narrow tucks at regular intervals.

Apart from muslin, checked cotton was also frequently used in Gustavian interiors, not only on windows but also for bed hangings and on seating. In the grandest homes of the late eighteenth century, fine silks were used for upholstering the loose squab seats and backs of armchairs; these were then covered with simple loose covers in checked cotton or linen. The daybed, with bolster cushions at each end, and sometimes a simple canopy, is another classic piece which often utilized checked cotton.

If you have an open, wasted area under the stairs, this could be an ideal place for a Gustavian-style daybed, providing useful extra seating in the hall. Make a simple gingham cover for a plain divan, and add bolster cushions at each end. If desired, make a canopy for the back and sides which is suspended from the underside of the stairs.

Bleached floorboards, painted wooden chairs with cushions, cool, matt colours, sheer curtains, and a gilt mirror work better in the hall than they would in virtually any other room, making it an ideal place to try Gustavian style for yourself.

Seat Cushion with Skirt

Painted wooden chairs with simple checked cushions were a hallmark of Gustavian style. This lightly padded cushion has a pleated "skirt" which fastens around the back strut, giving it a pretty, feminine look.

1 Lay the paper for the pattern over the chair seat. Use a pencil to mark around the outer edge of the seat. Remove from the seat. Fold the paper in half from front to back, and cut out around the marked outline. Replace on the seat to check for fit. Mark the position of the front corners, outer back struts and either side of the centre back strut.

2 Using the pattern, cut one piece from fabric and one from lining, adding a 1.5cm (⅝in) seam allowance all around. Cut one piece of wadding (batting).

3 Measure the seat for the skirt. Decide on the length of the skirt and add 3.5cm (1⅜in) for seam and hems. Measure around the seat from centre back to centre back; add 32cm (12½in) for centre front pleats, 32cm (12½in) for centre back pleats and 2.5cm (1in) for the back overlap fastening. Cut out one piece of fabric to this size.

4 Neaten the hem edge of the skirt and then turn it up for 1cm (⅜in); pin and stitch. Measuring from the centre of the skirt, form two 8cm (3⅛in) wide inverted pleats at each front corner and again at each back corner position. Tack (baste) across the top and base of the pleats to hold temporarily.

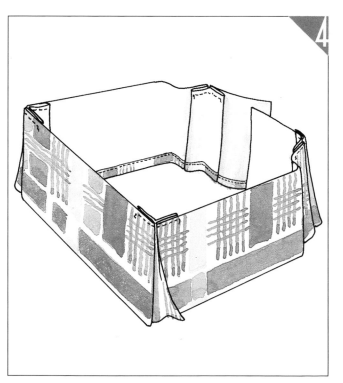

5 Make up sufficient covered piping cord to fit around the seat from the back on one side around to the back on the other side. Pin and tack to the fabric seat, neatening the ends of the piping.

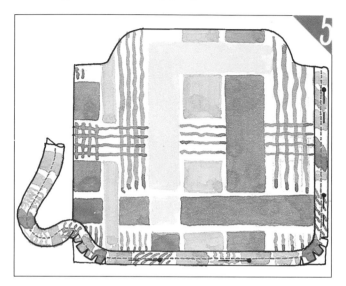

6 Make up two back tabs for fastening. Cut two pieces of fabric, each 10x8.5cm (4x3⅜in). Fold in half with right sides together; pin and stitch the raw edges together, leaving one end open. Trim and turn right side out. Topstitch across the end and down both side edges. Tack the tabs over the piping on either side of the centre back strut position.

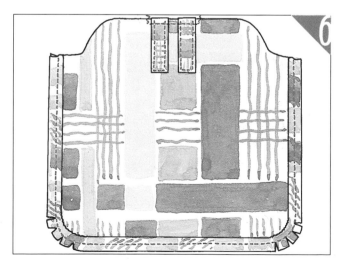

7 Position the skirt on the fabric cover over the piping, from the back strut position around the seat to the other back strut position. Pin and stitch, taking a 2.5cm (1in) seam allowance on the skirt and a 1.5cm (⅝in) allowance on the cover. Leave the remainder of the top of the skirt free.

8 Place the lining cover on the fabric cover with right sides together; pin and stitch all around, catching in the piping, skirt front and back tabs and leaving an opening. Trim and turn right side out. Insert wadding (batting) inside the cover, turn in the opening edges and slipstitch together to close.

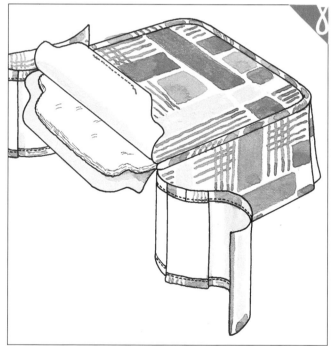

9 Neaten the top edge of the remaining skirt pieces by turning under 2.5cm (1in); pin and stitch the hem in place. Cut the length of the touch-and-close tape into small pieces. Place the cover on the chair seat; overlap the skirt at the back. Mark the positions, then stitch the touch-and-close tape in place to fasten the skirt ends together and to fasten them to both tabs.

Cased Sheer Curtains

The cool, airy look of simple sheer curtains is perfect for the Gustavian style interior. A single cased heading gives a suitably unfussy look. Because the heading is fixed, the curtains can be tied back or caught back over holdbacks attached to the wall.

1 For each curtain, measure from the curtain rod above the window to the floor and add 17cm (6¾in) for the top heading and base hem. Measure halfway across the rod and multiply by two or three, depending on the amount of fullness you require (sheer fabrics need more fullness than medium weight material); add 6cm (2½in) for side hems.

2 Make up each curtain in the same way. Cut out as many fabric widths as necessary to gain your required width. Pin and stitch the widths together with narrow flat-fell seams.

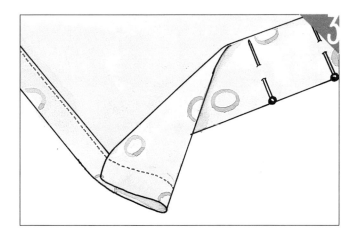

3 Turn under a double 1cm (⅜in) hem on both side edges; pin and stitch. Turn up a double 2.5cm (1in) hem across the base edge, forming neat corners. Pin and stitch the hems in place.

4 Turn down the top edge for 1cm (⅜in) and then for 5.5cm (2¼in). Pin and tack. Stitch across the curtain just above the hem edge and again 2.5cm (1in) down from top edge, to form a casing for the curtain pole and a self-frill above the pole.

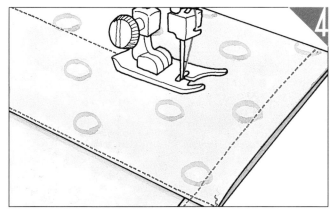

Materials Checklist
- ◉ *Sheer fabric*
- ◉ *Matching sewing thread*

5 Slide each curtain along the pole and fix back into place above the window. Drape the curtains back over holdbacks.

The Provencal Style Kitchen

THE HEART OF THE HOME, Provencal kitchens reflect the French love of cooking and eating. They are sparse and uncluttered, with solid, unfussy, practical furniture and tiled floors. The thick walls are colourwashed in warm tones of pink, apricot, pale ochre or cream, and the whole approach is functional and unpretentious; the precept "form follows function" is never more apparent than here. Meals are taken out-of-doors or at a solid wood table in the kitchen.

Soft furnishings do not feature heavily in the Provencal kitchen, but fabric can be used as curtains on cupboards, table linen and cushions. Window curtains should be made from simple muslin, cotton or lace in white or cream, or a Provencal print, hung from a thin wooden or brass pole.

Provencal prints are known all over the world. These bright, colourful cottons are an instantaneous way to evoke sunny Provence. The prints were first produced in Marseilles and Avignon about three hundred years ago, in imitation of the cotton chintzes imported from India. The prints were originally hand-blocked, and many of the original blocks have provided the basis for today's screen-printed Provencal cottons. Although synthetic dyes are used now, the colours are kept as similar to the original vegetable dyes as possible. Combined with geraniums, sunflowers and dried lavender, they bring a touch of Provence into any kitchen.

An ideal way to introduce a French flavour to your kitchen is to use several cushions in a Provencal print on a *banquette.* This is a simple seat which looks like two or three chairs joined together, with wooden arms at each end. The colourful cushions look great on it and also make the rush seat more comfortable.

Check gingham used on curtains inside the cupboard doors, and as a valance along the edge of a shelf, gives this kitchen a fresh, homely look.

The most important piece of furniture in the Provencal kitchen is the *armoire,* a large cupboard, often in walnut, with shelves for storing food or china.

The *armoire* too offers the opportunity to bring in some fabric, as the inside can look sensational lined with a bright Provencal fabric.

Squab cushions made from Provencal fabric, on chairs arranged around a large central table, create a French ambience in this kitchen. Gleaming copper pans and French pottery and enamelware add to the atmosphere.

*Cushions in
colourful Provencal
fabrics on a French
banquette provide
comfortable seating
and an instant
impression of the
South of France.*

Valance, Curtains & Tiebacks

This frilly valance, with complementary curtains and tiebacks, is the perfect foil to the rich tones of the wood in this kitchen. Restricting clutter to the valance shelf itself, leaving the rest of the kitchen bare, heightens the dramatic contrast.

Valance

1 To calculate the width of the valance, measure the valance rail, multiply the measurement by two and add 10cm (4in). For the depth, decide how deep you would like the valance to be, and add 7cm (2³/4in) for hems. Cut and join together enough fabric widths to make a piece of fabric to these measurements. Make up the lining in the same way but 7cm (2³/4in) narrower.

2 Place the fabric on the lining with right sides together; pin and stitch the side edges, taking a 1.5cm (⁵/8in) seam allowance. Press the seams open and, matching the centre, press the valance so a narrow hem of fabric forms on each end of the valance. Trim and turn right side out. Press.

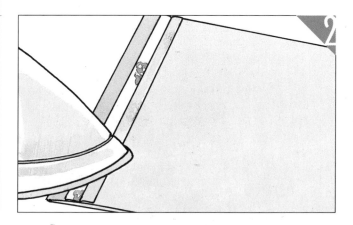

3 Turn up the base edge of the valance and turn under the base edge of the lining, so that the hemmed edge of the lining is slightly higher than the hemmed edge of the fabric; pin, tack and slipstitch the lining to the fabric across the hem edge.

4 Turn down the top edges together for 6.5cm (2¹/2in). Pin on the heading tape about 4cm (1¹/2in) below the top edge, to form a self-frill. Stitch both edges, stitching in the same direction, turning under both ends of the tape, and being careful to catch in the cords at one end but not at the other. Pull the cords to gather up the valance to the correct length. Knot the cords together and, if desired, wind the excess cord around a cord tidy. Insert hooks, and hang from the valance rail.

Curtains

1 For each curtain, measure half the curtain rail and multiply this measurement by one-and-a-half to two times, depending on the fullness you require. Measure the drop from the rail to the sill and add 3cm (1¼in) for seams. Join together fabric widths to make up a piece of fabric to the correct size. Repeat, to make up the lining in the same way.

2 Measure the side and base edges of the curtain and make up a length of covered piping cord to this length. Pin and tack (baste) piping cord around the fabric with the cord facing inwards and raw edges even. Neaten the ends of the piping.

3 For the frill, add the length of the curtain to the width. Multiply this measurement by four. Cut out 13cm (5¼in) wide strips and stitch together with flat-fell seams until you have a strip to this length. Turn under a double 1cm (³⁄₈in) hem on one long edge and both short edges of the frill; pin and stitch. Divide the frill into equal sections and work two rows of gathering stitches along the unhemmed long edge in each section in turn. (If you attempted to gather such a long section all at once, the threads would probably break.)

4 Divide up the side and base edges of the curtain into the same number of equal sections. Place the frill on the right side of the curtain, over the piping, matching the sections together and beginning and ending 1.5cm (⁵⁄₈in) down from the top edge. Pull up the gathers evenly in each section in turn. Pin and tack the frill in place on the curtains.

5 Place the lining on the curtain with right sides together. Pin and stitch the side and base edges, catching in the piping and the frill. Trim and turn the lined curtain right side out.

6 Turn down the top edges together for 1.5cm (⁵⁄₈in) and add heading tape, as for the valance but with the tape only 3mm (¹⁄₈in) inside the top edge. Insert hooks and hang from the curtain rail behind the valance.

Tiebacks

1 To work out the length of each tieback, hold a tape measure around the pulled-back curtain and make a note of the length.

2 For each tieback cut two 9cm (3¹⁄₂in) strips of fabric to the measured length plus 1.5cm (⁵⁄₈in).

3 Cut one piece of iron-on interfacing to the same size. Fuse this to the wrong side of one tieback piece.

4 For the frill, cut out 13.5cm (5¹⁄₂in) wide strips which when seamed together will be twice as long as the tieback. Pin and stitch the strips together with flat-fell seams. Turn under a 1cm (³⁄₈in) double hem on one long edge and both short edges of the frill; pin and stitch the hems in place.

5 Run two rows of gathering stitches along the unhemmed edge of the frill. With right sides together, pin the frill to one long edge of the interfaced tieback, 1.5cm (⁵⁄₈in) in from both short edges, and with raw edges even. Pull up the gathers evenly to fit; tack in place.

6 Place the second tieback on the first one with right sides together; pin and stitch all around, catching in the frill and leaving an opening centrally in one side. Trim and turn right side out. Turn in the opening edges and slipstitch to close.

7 Handsew a curtain ring to each end of the tieback so the rings just protrude over the side edges.

Novelty Cushions

Cushions in cheerful Provencal fabrics brighten up any room, and are ideal for a breakfast area. The design of these two cushions, one with a gathered edge and the other with a flamboyant frill and button opening, is in tune with the lighthearted feel of the fabrics.

Gathered edge cushion

Finished size: 35cm (14in) square

1 Cut two pieces of fabric each 38cm (15¼in) square. For covered piping, measure around the outer edge of one cushion piece. Cut out 7.5cm (3in) wide strips from across the fabric, which, when joined together, measure one and a half times the outside cushion measurement.

2 Fold the strip evenly in half around the cord. With a zip/piping foot on the sewing machine, stitch alongside the cord for approximately 20cm (8in). Stop

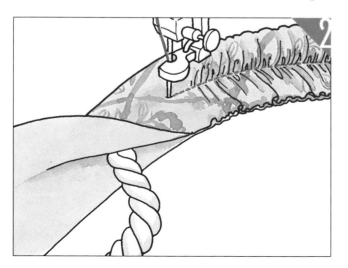

the machine with the needle in the fabric. Raise the presser foot and gently pull the cord to gather up the fabric. Lower the presser foot and continue stitching. Keep stopping and gathering up the fabric until you have covered all the cord.

3 Place the covered cord on the right side of one cushion piece, matching raw edges together and with the cord facing inwards. Join the fabric ends together to fit. Trim and butt join the cord ends, catching the ends together with a few hand stitches to hold them and prevent them from unravelling. Disguise the join by ruching up the fabric over the join. Pin and tack (baste) the piping in place.

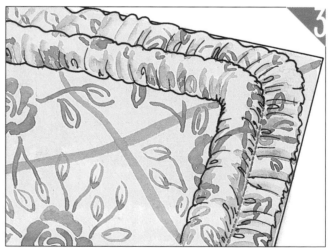

4 Place the second cushion piece on the first one with right sides together. Pin and stitch all around, leaving an opening in one side. Trim and turn right side out. Insert the cushion pad; turn in the opening edges and slipstitch together to close the opening.

Materials Checklist
✿ *60cm (³/₄yd) of 122cm (48in) wide Provencal print fabric*
✿ *1.60m (1³/₄yd) of thick piping or plain cord*
✿ *35cm (14in) square cushion pad*
✿ *Matching sewing thread*

Frilled cushion

Finished size: 40cm (16in) square excluding frill

1 For the back cut one piece 43cm (17¼in) square. For the front cut one piece 43x40cm (17¼x16in) and one piece 43x13cm (17¼x5in) and one strip 43x7.5cm (17¼x3in) for facing.

2 To work out the frill length, measure around the cushion back and add half as much again. Cut out 10.5cm (4¼in) wide strips from across the fabric width, which, when joined together, will be the desired frill length. Join the ends into a ring with a flat-fell seam.

3 Turn under a 1cm (³⁄₈in) hem on one edge of the facing strip; pin and stitch.

4 Make up a 38cm (15in) length of rouleau for button loops. Cut the rouleau into 9.5cm (3¾in) lengths. Form them into loops and pin to the narrow front section, evenly spaced approximately 6cm (2¼in) apart. Place the raw edge of the facing strip over the top with right sides together; pin and stitch, taking a 1.5cm (⁵⁄₈in) seam allowance. Turn right side out.

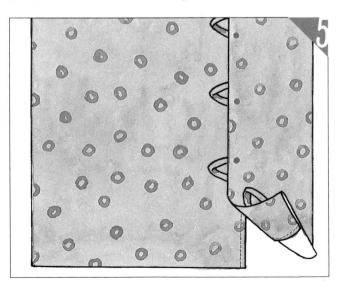

5 Stitch a 1cm (³⁄₈in) wide single hem on the wider front section. Turn under this edge for 5cm (2in); pin and tack. Place the fronts together, so the rouleau edge overlaps the wider front section by 2.5cm (1in); pin and tack together.

6 Turn under a double 6mm (¼in) hem along the base edge of the frill; pin and stitch in place. Work two rows of gathering along the opposite edge of the frill.

7 Pin the right side of the frill to the right side of the cushion front with the frill facing inwards and matching the raw edges together. Pull up the gathers evenly to fit around the cover, allowing extra fullness at each corner. Tack in place.

8 Place the cushion front on the back with right sides together. Pin and stitch all around, taking a 1.5cm (⁵⁄₈in) seam allowance. Trim and neaten the seam. Turn the cushion right side out through the front opening. Handsew the buttons to the wider front section to match up with the button loops. Alternate the button colours. Insert the cushion pad and fasten the buttons.

Materials Checklist

✿ 90cm (1yd) of 90cm (36in) wide Provencal print fabric
✿ Matching sewing thread
✿ 25mm (1in) diameter buttons, two in blue and two in yellow
✿ 40cm (16in) square cushion pad

Austrian Blind

Austrian blinds (shades) don't have to be fussy, as this stylish version proves. By choosing the right fabric, such as a Provencal print, and avoiding too much fullness, you can make a blind that is simple and chic.

I Fix a 25x25mm (1x1in) batten across the top of the window. The blind will be stapled to its top edge.

2 Measure the length of the batten and add 3cm (1¹/4in) for seams plus an extra 5cm (2in) for side hems. Measure the drop (to the window sill) and allow an extra 20cm (8in) for some fullness and 4cm (1¹/2in) for the top seam and the fixing. Pin and stitch the fabric widths together to gain the correct width measurement. Press the seams open. Repeat to make up the lining. Trim 5cm (2in) off each side of the lining.

3 Place the fabric on the lining with right sides together; the fabric will be wider than the lining. Pin and stitch the side edges together, taking a 1.5cm (5/8in) seam allowance. Press, matching the centres, so that a narrow hem of fabric forms on each side of the blind. Pin and stitch the base edges together. Trim and turn right side out. Turn the top edges to the inside; stitch.

4 Lay the blind flat, wrong side up. Mark 15cm (6in) from each side edge, then divide up the width in between into equal lengths approximately 120cm (48in) apart, to create the swags. Mark a vertical line up the blind at each marked position. Lay a length of Austrian blind tape on each marked line. Turn under the raw edges in line with the base edge of the blind, and position the first thread loop 5cm (2in) from the base

edge. Place a length of tape at each position, making sure that the thread loops match horizontally across the blind. Pin and stitch each length in place.

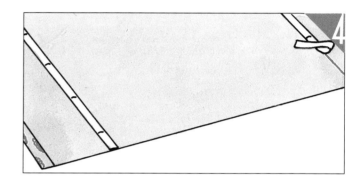

5 Cut a length of cord for each tape to twice the length of the blind and one width. Tie to the first thread loop at the base of the first tape. Thread the cord through all the loops above it. Repeat for each cord.

6 Fix a screw eye into the underside of the batten at each tape position and one at the outside edge. Tack the top edge of the blind and staple it to the top edge of the batten. Thread each cord through all the eyelets and out to the outside edge. Pull up the cords to ruche up the blind, knot together and wind around a cleat.

Placemats

Placemats are not, of course, typically French, but they do provide an excellent opportunity to introduce gorgeous Provencal fabric into the kitchen. These quilted placemats are simplicity itself to make and are fully washable.

1 Cut out an oval or rectangular pattern from paper, then use this to cut out two pieces of fabric and one piece of wadding (batting) for each mat.

2 Sandwich the wadding between the two pieces of fabric and tack together over the entire surface. Topstitch through all layers to quilt the placemat, either following the pattern of the fabric, or stitching in a grid pattern. Trim the edges of the fabric and wadding so they are even.

3 Cut 5cm (2in) wide strips of fabric on the bias and join them together with diagonal seams to make a strip long enough to bind all around each placemat. Fold the long raw edges in to the centre, and press.

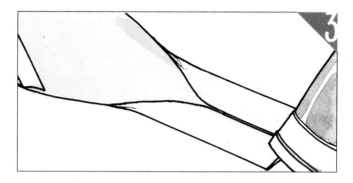

4 With right sides together, lay the bias binding on the front of the mat. Pin the raw edge of the binding around the raw edge of the placemat, turning under the ends. Stitch along the crease line of the binding through all thicknesses. Wrap the binding over to the back of the mat and turn under the other raw edge along the other crease line. Slipstitch neatly in place.

Materials Checklist

- ✿ *Provencal cotton fabric, for placemats*
- ✿ *Matching or contrasting fabric, for binding*
- ✿ *Lightweight wadding (batting)*
- ✿ *Matching sewing threads*

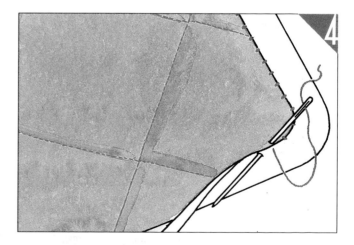

The Cottage Style Bedroom

W hat could be more charming in the bedroom than a cottage-style decor? Uncontrived, small-scale and informal, it has a cosy, snug feeling that is tailormade for the bedroom.

The furnishings are simple and practical rather than grand or ornate: here you'll find pine rather than mahogany; and muslin, gingham, ticking or sprigged cotton rather than damask or heavily patterned prints. (*Toiles de Jouy*, some chintzes and Provencal prints, which are all covered in other chapters because of their suitability to other rooms, are equally at home in the bedroom.)

Cottage windows tend to be small, which means that (a) they must not reduce the incoming light, and (b) they should not overwhelm the window either in size or in style. Simple sill-length curtains with a gathered heading, hung from a plain wooden, iron or brass pole, often look most appropriate. Lavish trimmings do not usually look right.

One charming and very easily achieved window treatment in a cottage-style bedroom is a panel of lace slotted onto a wire or narrow brass rod along the top of the window, within the recess. To open the curtain, simply loop it back over a holdback on the wall to one side of the window, leaving the cased heading in place.

Many cottage bedrooms are tucked under the roof and therefore have dormer windows. Curtaining these windows without seriously reducing incoming light can sometimes be a problem. One solution is to make double-sided curtains, or use a fabric that is the same on both sides, and hang these from hinged rods. They can be turned into the alcove in the daytime without reducing light at all, and at nighttime simply swivelled

back over the window. Tiebacks or holdbacks attached to the alcove walls will prevent the curtains from hanging down into the room.

As well as window and bed treatments, there are other ways to introduce textiles into a cottage-style bedroom without making it look too fussy or grand. For example, instead of a wardrobe for hanging clothes, utilize a suitably proportioned alcove by hanging a curtain over it.

It's not difficult to give an ottoman a loose fabric cover or make a simple cushion that fits the top of a blanket box. Other ideas for using fabric in the bedroom include a padded lining and seat cushion for a wicker, rattan or Lloyd Loom chair; a gusseted cushion to fit a window seat; a slip cover for a comfortable old armchair; a gathered screen; tablecloths for bedside tables; and a flat wall curtain with loops hanging from a Shaker-style pegboard (see page 115).

An essential element of the charm of cottage style is the faded look of old textiles, such as linen curtains and patchwork quilts. A tried-and-tested way of giving new

Create a half-tester effect for a bed under a low sloping ceiling, using a lacy fabric gathered onto one curtain rod and held back by a second.

Embroidery has an even longer history, with the earliest domestic embroidery being used to decorate household linen, furnishings and personal effects. Although some embroidery is very intricate and time-consuming, it is possible to create delightful effects on bed linen or other soft furnishings in next to no time, with no previous experience.

The bed can, in fact, be treated in any number of ways, with a multitude of possible styles for bedcovers, bed linen, valances, canopies, or cushions.

However, tempting as it is to introduce frills galore, try to remember that, traditionally, cottage bedrooms have always been sparsely furnished. To avoid a claustrophobic effect, err on the side of too little rather than too much.

LEFT: Florals and checks look just right in a cottage bedroom and can be combined quite boldly if the colours tone.

BELOW: Patchwork quilts, long associated with cottage bedrooms, are the perfect foil for either natural or painted wood.

fabrics this faded look is to use an infusion of tea to stain it. Soak the fabric in the strained tea for five to ten minutes, then rinse and dry it.

The largest item in the room, the bed is an important element in the soft furnishings. Here is the perfect opportunity to bring in needlecrafts like patchwork and embroidery. Patchwork has for centuries been worked by cottage dwellers, who put leftover scraps of fabric to good use making patchwork bedcovers. Scraps of the cotton chintzes imported from India three hundred years ago were much-coveted for this purpose.

By the nineteenth century, patchwork had become a craze enjoyed by rich and poor alike, and appeared on other soft furnishings such as seats, stools and tablecloths. Although it went out of favour early in the twentieth century, it has for the past few decades enjoyed renewed popularity.

Gathered Screen

Screens made from fabric gathered onto a hinged wooden frame look so attractive that it's worth inventing a function for one. In fact, they are highly practical as they can be used in any number of ways – in front of a window instead of curtains or a blind, concealing a wash basin, or defining an area of the room. For a cottage style bedroom choose a suitably fresh, simple fabric such as gingham, a small-sprigged print or muslin. If you want it to look good from both sides, choose a woven fabric, which will be the same on the right side as on the wrong side.

1 Measure one of the screen panels from rod to rod and add 16cm (6½in) for the top and base casings. Measure across one panel and allow half as much again. Cut out three pieces of the fabric to this measurement.

2 Turn under a double 1cm (³⁄₈in) wide hem down each side edge; pin and stitch.

3 Turn down 8cm (3¼in) at the top edge and then turn under the raw edge for 1cm (³⁄₈in); pin and stitch across the base and the top of the hem, to form a deep casing.

4 Repeat to hem the base edge of the panel in the same way. Repeat to make up the remaining screen panels in the same way.

5 Remove the rods from the screen and thread through the casings; replace on the screen.

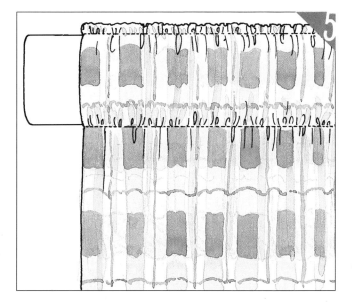

NOTE

If the rods cannot be removed from the screen, do not make a casing but instead turn under the raw edges of the panel for 1cm (³⁄₈in) and fold them over the rod; handsew the folded edges in place. Repeat for the base rods in the same way.

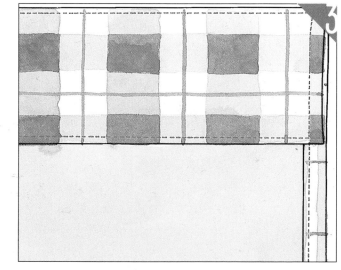

Materials Checklist
- ❈ *Folding screen frame*
- ❈ *Woven furnishing fabric*
- ❈ *Matching sewing thread*

Check Cushions

This fresh and pretty cushion trio would look good in any cottage bedroom, particularly on a wooden settle or an old-fashioned bedstead. Ribbons and lace add interest to the cheerful checks.

Red and blue cushion

Finished size: 38cm (15in) square

1 From fabric cut out one 41cm (16¼in) square for the cushion front and two pieces each 41 x 27.5cm (16¼x10¾in) for the cushion back.

2 Turn under a double 1cm (⅜in) wide hem along one long edge of each cushion back. Place the backs right side up and overlap the hemmed edges for 10cm (4in); tack (baste) together.

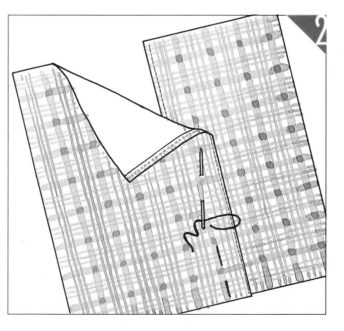

3 Lay out the cushion front. Mark a 16cm (6¼in) square around the centre. Turn under the raw edge of the broderie anglais trimming and place around the marked outline. Join the ends together to fit and mitre the corners. Pin and topstitch in place.

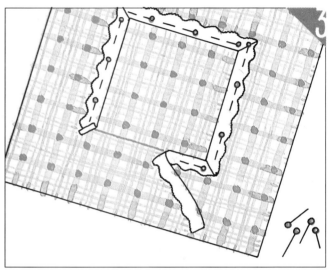

4 Position the lace edging around the outer edge of the cushion 1.5cm (⅝in) from the edge. Join the ends to fit and mitre the corners. Pin and topstitch in place.

5 Place the cushion front on the back with right sides together; pin and stitch, taking a 1.5cm (⅝in) seam. Trim and neaten the edges. Turn right side out.

6 Thread each length of ribbon through the eyelets in the lace on one side of the cushion, leaving an equal amount at each corner. Tie the ribbon ends together into bows at each corner. Trim the ends diagonally. Insert the cushion pad through the opening in the back.

Materials Checklist

✿ *50cm (¹/2yd) of 90cm (36in) wide yellow and white gingham fabric*
✿ *1.70m (1⁷/8yd) of 8cm (3³/8in) wide white lace edging with eyelet slots*
✿ *3m (3¹/4yd) of 5mm (¹/4in) wide yellow ribbon*
✿ *38cm (15in) square cushion pad*
✿ *Matching sewing threads*

Yellow cushion

Finished size: 38cm (15in) square

1 From fabric cut one 41cm (16¹/4) square of fabric for the front. Cut two pieces each 41 x 27.5cm (16¹/4x10³/4in) for the cushion back.

2 Form the back opening in the same way as for the ribbon-trimmed cushion, step 2.

3 Lay out the front, with right side uppermost. Position lace edging around the front with the inner edge 1.5cm (⁵/8in) in from the outer edge of the fabric. Join the ends together to fit, and mitre the corners. Pin and topstitch in place.

4 Place the cushion front on the back with right sides together. Pin and stitch together all around, being careful not to catch the lace in the seam. Trim and neaten the seam. Turn the cover right side out.

5 Cut the ribbon into four equal lengths. Thread each length through one side of the lace, leaving an equal length at each corner. Catch down the ribbon with a

few handstitches at each corner. Tie the ribbon ends into bows at each corner. Trim the ribbon ends diagonally. Insert the cushion pad through the opening in the back.

Rose-print cushion

Finished size: 38cm (15in) square

1 Centring the fabric design, cut one 41cm (16¹/4) square for the cushion front and two pieces each 41x27.5cm (16¹/4x10³/4in) for the cushion back.

2 Form the back opening in the same way as for the ribbon-trimmed cushion, step 2.

3 Place the cushion front on the back with right sides together; pin and stitch together all around, taking a 1.5cm (⁵/8in) seam allowance. Trim and neaten the seams. Turn right side out.

4 Lay the white trim around the outer edge of the cover, joining the ends together to fit and mitring the corners. Topstitch in place around the outer edge of the cushion. Insert the cushion pad through the opening.

Materials Checklist

✿ *50cm (¹/2yd) of 90cm (36in) wide printed fabric*
✿ *1.70m (1⁷/8yd) of 6.5cm (2¹/2in) wide white cotton lace trimming*
✿ *38cm (15in) square cushion pad*
✿ *Matching sewing threads*

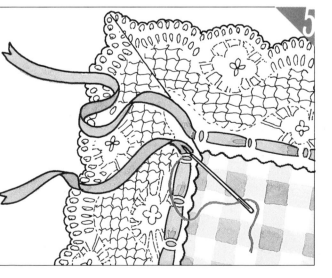

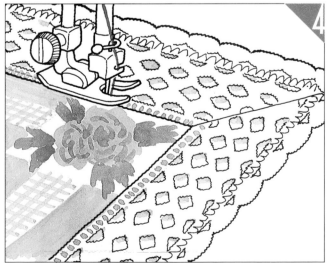

Embroidered Bed Linen

What could be nicer in a cottage bedroom than bed linen embroidered with simple cross-stitch flowers? Cross-stitch is so easy to do that someone who has never embroidered before can easily master it, and the scale of the motifs means they are quick to work. Using "waste canvas" enables you to embroider straight onto any fabric, including pure cotton or linen sheets and even antique bed linen.

Finished size (each motif): 6.5x5cm (2½x2in)

1 Tack (baste) across the centre of each piece of waste canvas both ways to find the centre point.

2 Lay out the sheet top flat and mark the position of each motif along the top edge, just below the hem. Space the motifs approximately 4cm (1½in) apart. At each position, centre a piece of waste canvas over the sheet and tack firmly in place.

3 The chart shows the sprig motif pointing in two directions, so you can pick the direction the motifs will lie across the sheet. Use three strands of embroidery cotton in the needle for all the stitching. Embroider each motif centrally on each piece of waste canvas in cross stitch, following the chart on page 91 for colours.

4 Fit each piece of canvas (with the sheet) into the hoop in turn to work the stitching. When working cross stitch, make sure you take the needle through the waste canvas and the sheet with each stitch. Cross-stitch can be worked from right to left or from left to right, but the diagonals must face in the same direction.

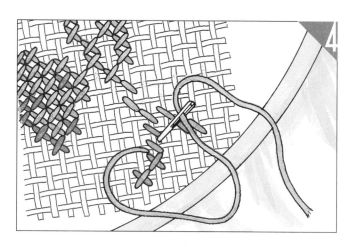

5 When the stitching is complete, remove the work from the hoop. Carefully snip the canvas threads and remove them from behind the embroidery, strand by strand. Use tweezers to help remove the strands.

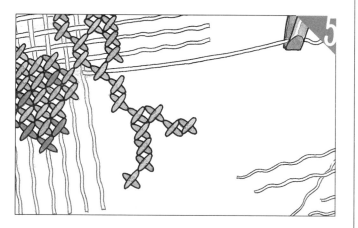

6 Gently press each motif on the wrong side being careful not to flatten the stitches.

7 Embroider each motif across the hem of the pillowcases in the same way as for the sheet.

Material Check List
- ❁ *Single-size flat sheet and two pillowcases*
- ❁ *Coats Anchor stranded embroidery cotton in the following colours: pale pink 1021, pale green 1043, green 243, pale yellow 301, pale rust 1002, deep rose 1023*
- ❁ *2cm (5in) squares of waste canvas with 14 threads to 2.5cm (1in) – about 20 for a single sheet, and about 5 for each pillowcase*
- ❁ *Embroidery needle*
- ❁ *Embroidery hoop*

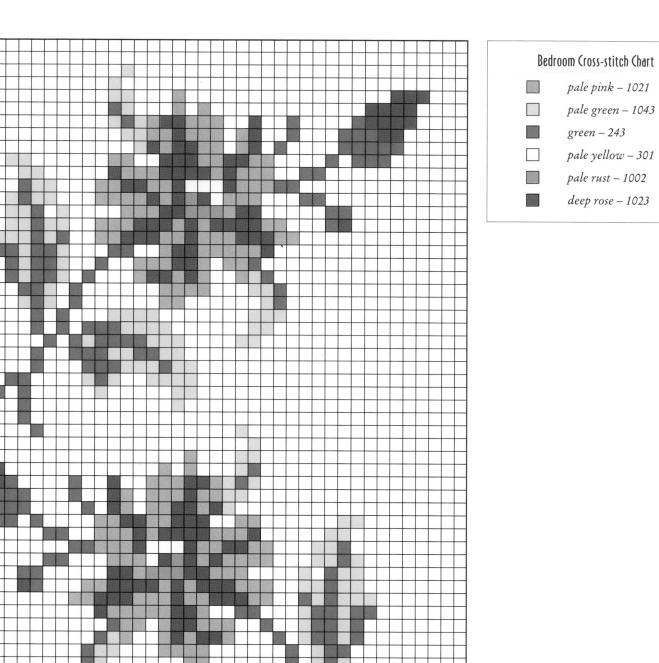

Bedroom Cross-stitch Chart

- pale pink – 1021
- pale green – 1043
- green – 243
- pale yellow – 301
- pale rust – 1002
- deep rose – 1023

Tea-towel Bedspread

It's hard to believe that this splendid bedspread has been made from tea towels. In fact, twelve French jacquard tea towels were simply sewn together, patchwork style, and fringing added around the edges. This type of tea towel is heavy enough that a very substantial bedspread is produced, and the rustic design makes it perfect for cottage style bedrooms.

Finished size: 315x185cm (124x73in), to fit a single bed

1 Carefully unpick the hems all around each tea towel and press flat. Place all the towels together and check that the sizes are the same. If not, stretch and press each towel over a damp cloth, until they are all the same size.

2 Lay out the tea towels flat so there are four rows of three, with the design running in the same direction.

3 Pin and stitch the towels together, following the original stitching lines. Begin by stitching the towels together into horizontal rows. Place the first two towels with right sides together and raw edges even; pin and stitch one long edge. Then pin and stitch the third towel to the opposite edge. Press the seams open. Repeat to make up the four rows in the same way.

4 When all the rows are stitched together; pin and stitch the rows together to form the complete bedspread. Make sure that all the seamlines match across the bedspread.

5 Turn under the outer edges all around the bedspread, following the original lines to form a narrow double hem; pin and stitch.

6 Pin the fringing around the side and base edges of the bedspread, so the edge of the fringe just overlaps the edge of the bedspread. Tuck under the raw ends of the fringe at each side of the top edge, to neaten. Pin and topstitch the fringing in place.

Materials Checklist
✪ *Twelve French jacquard tea towels each 77x55cm (30x21½in)*
✪ *Matching sewing thread*
✪ *8m (8¾yd) of 10cm (4in) wide white cotton fringing*

Bed Canopies

Bed hangings needn't be elaborate – sometimes a simple treatment looks most effective, particularly in a cottage style bedroom. Here, two styles of canopy are shown – a soft, gathered-up one of sheer, floaty muslin, and a more tailored one of checked furnishing cotton. Either can be suspended from brackets, or long curtain holdbacks, attached to the wall above the bedhead, near the ceiling. Alternatively, you could fix the central bracket near the ceiling and the two side brackets lower down, to create a triangular-shaped canopy.

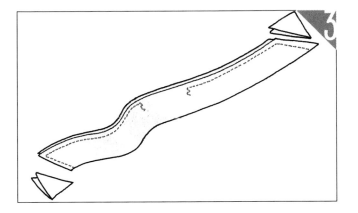

Finished size: to fit across a double bed placed at right angles to the wall, or a single bed placed lengthwise against the wall

Materials Checklist

❂ 150cm (60in) wide sheer muslin or 114cm (45in) wide checked fabric (or other heavy furnishing cotton)
❂ Lining fabric (for checked canopy)
❂ Matching sewing thread
❂ 3 brackets or curtain holdbacks, each about 30-35cm (12-14in) long
❂ Touch-and-close tape (optional)

1 Fix the brackets or holdbacks on the wall above the head of the bed, near the ceiling. Measure from the centre bracket out to one outside bracket and to the floor at the side of the bed. Add 2cm (3/4in) for hems. Double this measurement to get the length of the canopy, whichever style you are having.

2 For the muslin canopy, cut a piece of sheer fabric to this length, using the full width. Turn under a narrow 6mm (1/4in) double hem on the side edges of the canopy; pin and stitch in place. Turn up a double 1cm (3/8in) hem on both ends of the canopy; pin and stitch in place.

3 For the muslin ties, cut two pieces 150x25cm (60x10in). Fold each tie in half lengthwise, with right sides together. Diagonally cut across both short ends. Pin and stitch the raw edges together, taking a 1.5cm (5/8in) seam allowance and leaving an opening centrally

in the long side. Trim and turn right side out. Turn in the opening edges and slipstitch to close.

4 For the checked canopy, cut the fabric into a strip as wide as the brackets plus 2cm (3/4in), and the length calculated in step 1. Cut a strip of lining fabric to the same size. With right sides together and raw edges even, stitch the checked fabric and lining together along all four edges, taking a 1cm (3/8in) seam allowance. Turn right side out through the opening. Press, and slipstitch the opening to close.

5 Place the canopy (either bunched-up for the muslin, or flat for the checked fabric) on the brackets. You may wish to secure it to the brackets with a little touch-and-close tape.

HINT

On directional patterns, cut the fabric in two halves and rejoin with a flat-fell seam at the centre top, so the pattern will run up towards the centre of the canopy. Complete in the same way as before.

The Modern Style Bedroom for Kids

B RIGHT COLOURS and streamlined, modern furnishings are perfect for children of all ages, from babies and toddlers to teens.

Very young children love the stimulation bright primary colours offer, and many of the toys, items of furniture and accessories such as lamps, pictures and toy boxes available today are in these colours. Choosing similar colours, or white accented with primaries, makes it easier to create a harmonious, coordinated effect.

Plastic doesn't look out of place in this type of decor and, as there are some very well-designed plastic items available for young children, it makes sense to choose a style where they can be incorporated. Nostalgic, Edwardian-style nurseries do undeniably look lovely,

PRECEDING SPREAD:
A novelty print
fabric can be used
in lots of ways in a
child's room.

RIGHT:
Different checks
can often be
combined
successfully.

but are much more restricting in the furnishings you can include.

As children get older they develop tastes of their own and also start to like the same things their friends do – which may not always coincide with your own taste. Once again, a modern decor is likely to accommodate the character merchandising, posters, stickers, snapshots and other ephemera that they cannot live without.

By the teens the toys will have been replaced with hi-fi equipment and more sophisticated study aids. Once again, a modern style will prove infinitely adaptable and is much more likely to be along the lines of how the teenager wants his or her room to look.

BELOW: Brightly contrasting trim on simple white tab curtains sharpens up a modern all-white scheme in a teenager's bedroom.

Ethnic elements such as kilims or dhurries can be introduced to add warmth and textural interest.

Soft furnishings offer the chance to add colour and at the same time soften the look, since modern decor can look rather hard and clinical without fabric. Simple, fun curtains or blinds (shades), novel cushions and cheerful bedspreads or duvet covers can all look fabulous in a lively modern style.

Pick up the colours of soft furnishings in paintwork and in accessories.

Animal-patterned fabrics, so popular with children, can look stylish if carefully chosen.

Duvet Cover

A duvet cover is simplicity itself to make, and adding a complementary border makes it much more attractive. You could carry the theme onto the window by using the same fabric on a border all around each curtain as in this photograph. (Instructions for making curtains with ties, which are similar to those shown here, are on page 47.)

Finished size: 200x140cm (79x55in).

1 For the back, cut two pieces of check sheeting, one measuring 143x16.5cm (56¼x6½in) and one 143x199cm (56¼x78⅝in).

2 For the front border, cut two strips each 203x13cm (78¾x5¼in) and two strips each 143x13cm (56¼x5¼in). Fold up the end of each strip diagonally to meet the opposite edge; press. Unfold and cut across the diagonal press line.

Materials Checklist
❂ *Piece of patterned sheeting 183x123cm (72x48½in)*
❂ *2.20m (2½yd) of 228cm (90in) wide check sheeting*
❂ *Large press fasteners (snaps)*
❂ *Matching sewing thread*

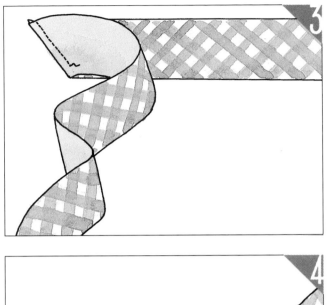

3 Place the border strips together in order: long, short, long and short, with right sides together; pin and stitch the ends together, taking a 1.5cm (⅝in) seam allowance and ending the stitching 1.5cm (⅝in) from the inner edges. Trim and press the seams open.

4 Place the border on the patterned sheeting with right sides together. Pin and stitch together all around. At each corner the border seam will open to help stitch smoothly around the corner. Press the border flat.

5 Turn under a double 2.5cm (1in) hem along one edge of each duvet back piece; pin and stitch. Place the backs with right sides up. Overlap the hemmed edges; pin and tack together.

6 Place the back and front duvet sections with right sides together; pin and stitch together all around. Trim and neaten the seams together. Turn the duvet right side out through the opening at the back. Press.

7 Handsew the press fasteners (snaps) to either side of the hemmed opening, spacing them approximately 18cm (7in) apart.

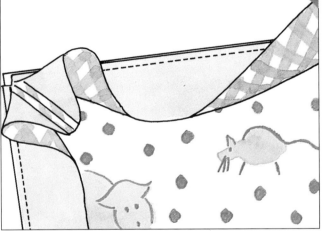

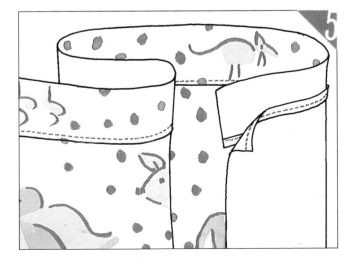

Geometric Cushions

Children will love these bold, bright, sturdy cushions. The unusual trim – cord threaded through jumbo eyelets – adds to the strong graphic look.

Red cushion

Finished size: 50cm (20in) square including border

1 From fabric cut two pieces each 53cm (21¼in) square for cushion front and back.

2 Place cushion pieces with right sides together; pin and stitch all around, taking a 1.5cm (⅝in) seam allowance and leaving an opening in one side. Trim and turn right side out.

3 Topstitch all around the cover 5cm (2in) and again 5.5cm (2¼in) away from the outer edges, leaving an opening in both rows of stitching in the same side as the opening in the outer edge.

4 Measure and mark the positions of four eyelets in two opposite sides. Position them centrally in the border and spaced approximately 15cm (6in) apart. Fix an eyelet at each marked position.

5 Insert the cushion pad; turn in the opening edges in the outer edge and slipstitch to close. Topstitch across the inner opening, matching up the two previous rows of topstitching.

6 Cut the piping cord into two equal lengths. Take the first length and knot one end. Thread the cord through the four eyelets across one side. Knot the opposite end of the cord. Repeat with the second length through the opposite eyelets.

Materials Checklist

✿ 60cm (¾yd) of 114cm (45in) wide printed cotton fabric
✿ Eight brass-coloured eyelets 15mm (⅝in) in diameter plus eyelet tool
✿ 1.10m (1¼yd) of thick piping cord
✿ 40cm (16in) square cushion pad
✿ Matching sewing threads

Yellow cushion

Finished size: 46cm (18in) square including border

1 From fabric cut out two 49cm (19¼in) squares of fabric for cushion front and back.

2 Make up the cushion in the same way as for the red cushion but with only one row of topstitching around the 5cm (2in) wide border.

3 Measure and mark the eyelet positions centrally in the border, 10cm (4in) on either side of each corner. Cut the cord into four equal lengths. Thread the cord across the corners and knot the ends together.

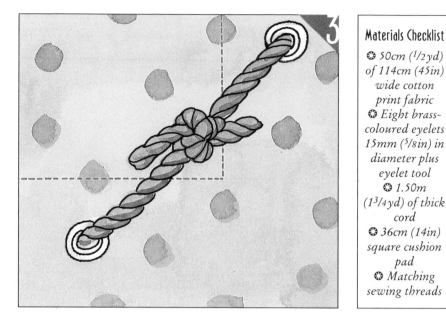

Materials Checklist

✪ 50cm (½yd) of 114cm (45in) wide cotton print fabric
✪ Eight brass-coloured eyelets 15mm (⅝in) in diameter plus eyelet tool
✪ 1.50m (1¾yd) of thick cord
✪ 36cm (14in) square cushion pad
✪ Matching sewing threads

Green and white stripe cushion

Finished size: 48cm (19in) square including border

1 For the back cut one 51cm (20¼in) square. For the front cut two strips each 54x27cm (21½x10¾in).

2 To make up the front, cut the two strips in half. Pin and stitch the two halves together with the stripes lying in opposite directions. Press the seam open. Pin and stitch the two halves together, to form the complete front. Press the seam open.

3 Complete the cushion cover in the same way as for the red cushion cover, but topstitch around the outside edge following the width of the fabric stripe.

4 Following the manufacturer's instructions, cover the button with an offcut of fabric and handsew to the centre of the cushion.

Materials Checklist

✪ 60cm (¾yd) of 114cm (45in) wide striped fabric
✪ One 40mm (1½in) diameter self-covering button
✪ 42cm (16½in) square cushion pad
✪ Matching sewing threads

Patchwork Bedspread

This is patchwork with a difference. Big, bold patches of colourful check fabrics look sensational in a child's bedspread, and make it very quick to run up.

Finished size: 270x180cm (106x70in).

1 From each of the print fabrics cut six 33cm (13¼in) squares. This includes a seam allowance.

2 Lay all the squares out on a flat surface, so there are six squares across the width and nine squares down the length. Move the different squares about until the arrangement looks good. Pin and stitch a line of nine squares together to form the first vertical row, taking a 1.5cm (⅝in) seam allowance. Repeat for the other vertical rows of squares. Press the seams open.

3 Lay out the strips, and pin them together vertically to form the bedspread, being careful to match the seams across each join. Stitch all the seams.

4 Cut two 273cm (107¼in) lengths of interlining. Lay the two lengths side by side. Just overlap the long edges and zigzag stitch together over the join. Trim to match patchwork.

5 Cut two 273cm (107¼in) lengths of lining. Place with right sides together; pin and stitch one long edge. Press the seam open. Trim to match patchwork.

6 Place the patchwork flat, wrong side up, and lay the interlining over the top, matching the outer edges. Pin and tack (baste) together.

Materials Checklist
❁ 70cm (¾yd) of 102cm (40in) wide cotton fabric in nine different patterns
❁ 5.50m (6yd) of 102cm (40in) wide woollen interlining
❁ 5.50m (6yd) of 102cm (40in) wide plain cotton for backing
❁ Matching sewing threads

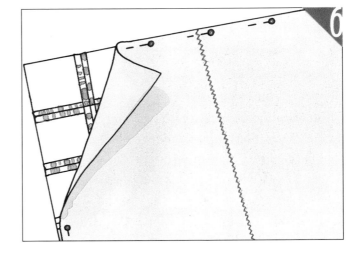

7 Place the lining on the patchwork with right sides together; pin and stitch together all around, leaving an opening in one edge. Trim the seams and turn right side out. Turn in the opening edges and slipstitch. Press.

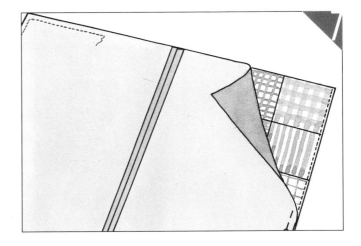

8 If necessary to prevent the lining from moving away from the patchwork, topstitch around some squares, stitching in the seamline.

Bed Valance

A simple pleated bed valance is tailored enough for a boy's room (and would in fact look smart in a girl's bedroom too). With a check like this you have to match the pattern, but the effect is worth the extra effort. If you are using a fairly expensive fabric, you could economize by substituting a cheap plain fabric for the main part, since only the skirt will actually show.

1 Removing all the bedclothes and the mattress, measure the bed base. For the main top panel measure the length and width of the bed base and add a 3 cm (1¼in) seam allowance to the width and 3.5cm (1⅜in) to the length. For the skirt measure both the long and one short edge and allow for three times this measurement for the pleats plus 4cm (1½in) for the top side hems.

2 Cut out one main piece. Curve the two base corners by placing a plate on each base corner so that the edges are touching and draw around it. Cut out along the marked line.

Materials Checklist
❁ Sheeting
❁ Matching
sewing thread

3 For the skirt cut out sufficient fabric strips to the correct depth which when joined together will be the correct length. Be sure to allow for matching the pattern if necessary. Pin and stitch the strips together with narrow flat-fell seams.

4 Turn under a double 2.5cm (1in) wide hem along the lower edge of the skirt; pin and stitch.

5 Mark out 8cm (3¼in) wide knife pleats along the top and the hemmed edges of the skirt. Fold up the pleats and pin and tack across the top edge and the base edge.

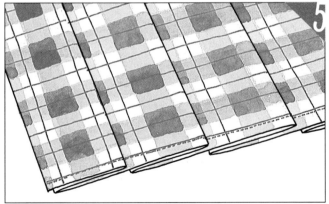

6 With the right sides together the raw edges level and the ends of the skirt to top edges of main panel pin the skirt to the main section. Check that the pleats fit all around and adjust as necessary, placing any smaller pleats on either side of the top edge. Pin and stitch together. Neaten the seams together.

7 Turn under a double 1cm (⅜in) hem across the top edge of the main panel and the skirts; pin and stitch.

The Colonial Style Bathroom

A COLONIAL STYLE BATHROOM is, of course, a contradiction in terms, since colonial American homes obviously did not have bathrooms, only perhaps a tin bath in front of the kitchen fire. Nevertheless, the style is eminently suitable for a bathroom and can be adapted to it very easily.

"Colonial" refers to the style found in the American colonies until after the War of Independence in the late eighteenth century, when the Federal style emerged. Because the colonists came from different countries, colonial style covers a very broad area, with many regional differences.

The style emerged from the settlers' desire to make a "home from home" in the New World. They wanted to recreate the styles of their mother country, but were forced to improvise and adapt because they had been able to bring very little with them. Many of the features most characteristic of colonial style, such as stencilling and rag rugs, originated in the attempt to dress up the very basic materials they had to hand.

Painted wood, tongue-and-groove panelling (known as matchboarding) and floorboards stencilled or painted and covered with stencilled floorcloths, are features of colonial style that are well suited to the bathroom. Sanitaryware should be simple and white, but a gingham skirt around the basin is very much in the colonial spirit.

Window treatments should be simple, with plain wooden, iron or dull brass poles, and fabrics natural. Cotton, muslin, gingham, cotton-linen unions and rough homespun cotton are all very suitable fabrics. Louvred shutters are also very much in keeping.

Finishing touches would include antique-effect samplers, Shaker boxes or (very much at home in the bathroom) decoy ducks.

Today the Shakers are closely associated with colonial style, and much passes for "Shaker" that is really a travesty of that style. Nevertheless, an amalgam of colonial and Shaker style can look superb in today's home. This light, airy, uncluttered look is particularly suited to the bathroom – as is the Shaker's philosophy of spotless cleanliness! (The Shaker's founder, Mother Ann Lee, claimed that "Good spirits will not live where there is dirt – there is no dirt in Heaven.")

The Shakers were an American religious sect, founded in the late eighteenth century. By the early nineteenth century they numbered around 6000, but from then on their numbers declined. There are fewer than a dozen Shakers today.

For a really authentic Shaker look, you need large uncurtained sash (double-hung) windows with small panes, polished wood floors, whitewashed walls, a wooden pegboard and painted or stained woodwork and cupboards (preferably built-in) – and very little else!

However, it is perfectly possible to adapt elements of Shaker style to your own home even if you don't have, say, sash windows or wooden floorboards. Nor do you have to banish all non-Shaker items from the home. The secret is to try to go along with the spirit of Shaker style,

which means that simplicity, order, harmony and utility are paramount. Superficial decoration and clutter should be eliminated, and only functional objects with clean, graceful lines should be used.

You could perhaps paint your walls white or off-white and doors, door and window frames, skirtings (baseboards), panelling, and bathroom cabinet in a typically Shaker colour – such as brown, red, ochre, sage green or the colour most associated with the Shakers, a deep slightly greenish blue.

A pegboard – a wooden rail with pegs, which runs around the room at about shoulder height – is a hallmark of Shaker style. The Shakers used the pegboards for hanging items like tools, chairs, baskets, brooms, clocks, candle sconces, cloaks and bonnets neatly out of the way. In the bathroom a pegboard provides a marvellous place to hang dressing gowns, a mirror, a drawstring bag, towels, backbrushes and other functional items. Avoid the temptation to clutter it up with purely decorative items.

The Shakers made their own homespun linen and wool, which was either plain, striped or checked. A wonderful selection of Shaker-type check fabrics is available today, and they look good as simple curtains. Roller blinds would also look suitable, but pelmets, ruffles or trimmings are out of character.

This is where you might prefer to abandon the Shaker style and opt for colonial style. Homespun checks and cafe curtains are widely used in colonial style homes too, but there is also a place for flower prints, frills and valances, so long as the effect is still simple and unsophisticated. Woven or braided rag rugs are typical of both colonial and Shaker style.

The other object that instantaneously says "Shaker" is the distinctive oval wooden box with its swallowtail joints. The Shakers made these in a variety of sizes and colours and used them for storing all manner of items. With a few Shaker boxes and a pegboard, your storage needs would be virtually taken care of.

PRECEDING SPREAD: The furnishings in a Shaker "retiring room", or bedroom, could just as well be used in a modern colonial style bathroom.

OPPOSITE: White painted walls, match-boarding and floorboards give this bathroom a colonial feeling. The tailored skirt around the vanity unit looks soft without being at all fussy.

Basin Skirt

In the bathroom a basin skirt offers a good way to introduce fabric, which helps to offset the hard, clinical look bathrooms often have. It is also very practical, as it provides an excellent storage area inside. Check gingham is the obvious choice for any colonial-style bathroom as it not only looks fresh but is historically authentic too.

1 Fix a covered wire around the basin top, on a hook inserted into the wall on each side of the basin. Measure the length of the wire and allow for one and a half times this measurement. Measure from the basin to the floor and add a total allowance of 10cm (4in) for the top heading and the hems.

2 Turn under a double 1cm (³⁄₈in) hem down each side; pin. Turn up a double 2.5cm (1in) wide hem along the base edge; pin. To form an uneven mitre at each corner, place a pin in the side edges where the base hem falls and in the base edge where the side hems fall. Unfold one hem width on both side and base edges; turn in the corner from pin to pin and then refold the hems over the turned-in corner. Pin and stitch the hems all around the curtain.

3 Turn down 5cm (2in) along the top edge, and tuck under 1cm (³⁄₈in); pin and stitch along the hem edge and again 1.5cm (⁵⁄₈in) above the first row of stitching to form a casing.

4 Thread the covered wire through the casing, ruching up the fabric. Rehang the curtain arranging the gathers evenly along the wire.

Materials Checklist
- ❀ *Furnishing fabric*
- ❀ *Matching sewing thread*
- ❀ *Covered curtain wire*

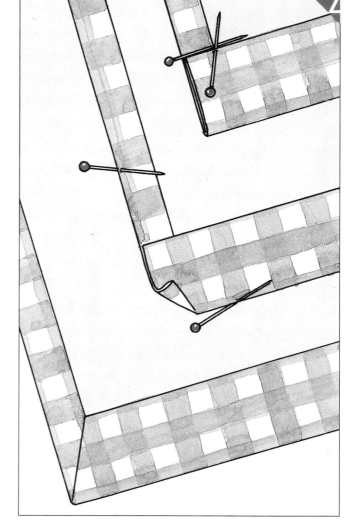

Tab Curtains

Simple tab-headed curtains in muslin or voile are a highly authentic window treatment in a colonial style room. The tabs here are part of the curtain, rather than being stitched on. If desired, a blind (shade) could be fixed to the window for added privacy.

1 Measure for each curtain: for the length measure from the curtain pole to the skirting (baseboard) and add 36.5cm (14½in) for the hems, tabs and seams. For the width, measure the length of the curtain pole and add 5cm (2in) for the side hems. Cut out two pieces of fabric to this size.

2 Make up each curtain in the same way. First make a paper pattern for the shaped top. Work out how many tabs will fit across the curtain top – allow about 14cm (5¼in) for the square gaps and about 8cm (3¼in) for the tabs. Divide the width of the curtain by 22cm (8½in) to find how many will fit across the curtain top, then add one more tab so there is a tab at each end. Adjust the amounts for all the gaps and check that all the tabs are the same size.

3 Draw up a template of one finished gap to the chosen width less 2cm (¾in) and 26.5cm (10½in) deep. Lay out one curtain, wrong side up. Measure in by the tab width plus 2cm (¾in) from one edge, then position the template and mark around it. Leaving a space equal to the gap plus 2cm (¾in), mark around the template again. Keep measuring and marking around the template across the complete curtain. The last rectangle you mark should be the same distance from the edge as the first one was.

4 Cut a 32cm (12½in) deep facing from the same fabric. Turn up 1cm (³⁄₈in); pin and stitch. Place the facing on the curtain top with right sides together. Pin and stitch around each gap and tab, taking a 1cm (³⁄₈in) seam allowance. Trim and turn right side out.

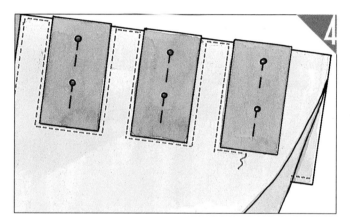

5 Turn under a double 5mm (¼in) side hem in line with the curtain top; pin and stitch. Turn up 10cm (4in) along the base edge, tuck under the raw edges, and pin and stitch.

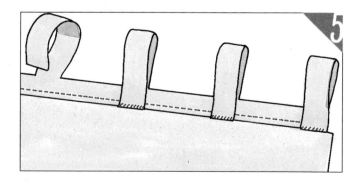

6 Fold the tabs in half and handsew the ends to the base of the facing.

Unlined Café Curtains

Scalloped café curtains are probably the most authentic-looking of all window treatments for a colonial-style room, particularly if you use a Shaker-type check fabric. Although often associated with the kitchen, they are ideal for the bathroom, as they provide privacy without blocking out the light.

1 For each curtain, measure across half the curtain pole, add 15cm (6in) and then multiply that figure by one and a half. (Café curtains should not be too full.) For the length, measure from the pole to the point at which the curtains will finish, and add 33cm (13in) to this measurement, plus one pattern repeat for each width after the first.

2 Cut out as many fabric widths as necessary. Trim off the selvedge edges, and join the fabric widths together with flat-fell seams. Press a double 7.5cm (3in) hem along the lower edge, and a double 4cm (1½in) hem along each side edge. Either hand sew or machine stitch, mitring the corners (see page 13).

3 Now plan the scalloped heading. Ideally the scallops should be 10-15cm (4-6in) across. They will not extend into the side hems, so subtract 7.5cm (3in) from the width of each curtain, then divide that figure by the approximate width of the scallops. Round the result up or down to a whole number. This is the number of scallops you will have in one curtain. The gaps between the scallops should be about 2.5cm (1in), and the number of gaps will be one less than the number of scallops. Therefore the space taken up by the gaps will be 2.5cm (1in) multiplied by the number of gaps. Subtract this amount from the total width the scallops and gaps will cover. Finally, divide by the number of scallops – this gives you the exact width of a scallop.

4 For example, if your curtain is 100cm (39in) wide you deduct 7.5cm (3in), which equals 92.5cm (36in). If you want the scallops to be about 15cm (6in), divide 92.5cm (36in) by 15cm (6in), which means you can have 6 scallops. Allowing for 5 gaps, each of which is 2.5cm (1in) wide, means you have to deduct 12.5cm (5in) from the overall width (excluding side hems) of 92.5cm (36in); you are left with 80cm (31in). Dividing this by 6 scallops gives you an exact diameter for each scallop of 13.3cm (5⅙in).

5 To make a pattern for the scallops, cut a strip of paper to the width of the curtain (excluding side hems) and 25cm (10in) deep. Fold it in half lengthwise. Using a pair of compasses, draw a series of semi-circles to the diameter you have calculated, spacing them 2.5cm (1in) apart, which is the width of the gaps, and starting and ending on the foldline.

Materials Checklist

✿ *Furnishing fabric*
✿ *Matching sewing thread*
✿ *Dressmaker's carbon paper and tracing wheel*
✿ *Curtain rings*

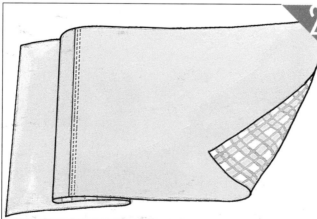

6 Measuring from the lower hemmed edge, mark the top of the curtain with a line of pins on the wrong side. Turn under 2.5cm (1in) on the top edge, and stitch. Now, with right sides together, fold the top along the line you marked with pins, to make a facing about 15.5cm (6in) deep. Remove the pins marking the line; press the fold.

7 Pin the template onto the facing, with the foldlines even, and the template centred between the side edges. Transfer the scalloped line to the fabric using a tracing wheel and dressmaker's carbon. Remove the template, and pin along the scallops. Stitch along the marked line.

8 Trim the seam allowance above the stitched scallops to 6mm (¹/₄in) and carefully clip the curves and across the corners.

9 Turn right side out and press. Handsew the sides of the facing to the side hems, and the lower edge of the facing to the curtain itself.

10 Attach a ring centrally between each scallop, and at the sides, either by sewing the rings to the fabric, or by clipping them on if you are able to obtain clip-on curtain rings.

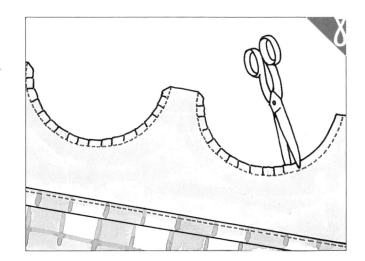

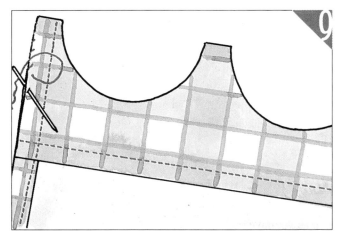

Rag Rug

Braided rugs are synonymous with colonial America. Thick, heavy wool was often used, but as a bathroom rug needs to be washable, Shaker checked cottons have been used here, with fleece interlining added for bulk. Instead of the overall mottled pattern used here, you may prefer the traditional look using bands of colour. To obtain these, several "rounds", or coils, are done in the same fabrics. Experiment with the different effects you can achieve by using, say, all three strips of the braid in the same colour, or two strands in a plain colour and one in check, or each strand in a different fabric. Traditionally no more than one strand is changed with each round, to get a softer transition between rounds.

1 From each fabric cut 8.5cm (3³/₈in) wide strips. To prepare each strip, feed it through the trimming and tape maker, and as the folded strip emerges, press well. If you don't have one of these, turn in both edges to almost meet in the centre; press well.

2 From iron-on fleece, cut out one 2.5cm (1in) wide strip to the same length as each strip of fabric. Open out each folded fabric strip and fuse a strip of fleece down the centre of the wrong side. Refold the strip around the fleece. Finally press each strip in half again, matching the folded edges.

3 Before you begin the rug, join several strips together ready for braiding. To do this, unfold the ends of two strips. Place them with right sides together; pin and stitch diagonally across the end. Trim the fabric and press the seam open. Trim the fleece so the edges butt together over the join. Refold and press the strips.

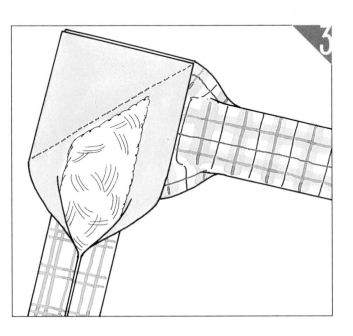

4 To begin the braid, unfold one strip at the join. Position the end of a third (folded) strip centrally over the join; stitch together.

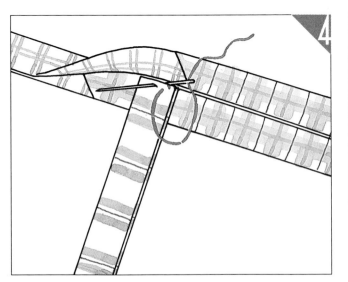

Materials Checklist

✺ *Selection of Shaker-type check cotton fabrics*
✺ *Iron-on fleece*
✺ *5cm (2in) trimming and tape maker (optional)*
✺ *Strong neutral-coloured sewing thread and needle*

5 Refold the unfolded strips and take the centre strip over the horizontal strip and down.

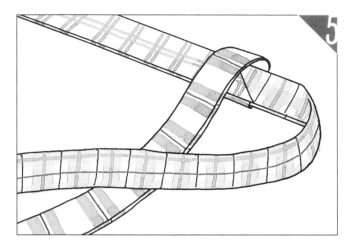

6 Begin the braid by taking the right-hand strip over the centre and then the left-hand strip over the centre. Continue in this way working a conventional three-strand braid. Adjust the braid as you go, making sure that the width remains the same and the strips lie flat.

7 Join in new strips as you braid by diagonally stitching together as in step 3. Use a clothes peg (clothespin) to hold the braid while you add the new strips.

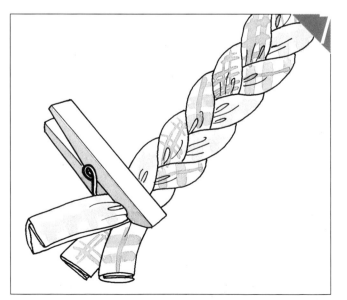

8 When you have a braid approximately 180cm (72in) long, you can begin to form the rug. Lay out 30cm (12in) of the braid for the centre. Then simply coil the braid around this strip. (Or, if you want a round rug, instead of oval, begin coiling right at the end of the braid.) Thread an embroidery needle with a double length of strong sewing thread; knot the end. Take the needle through the side of the braid, hiding the knot.

9 Lace the braid together taking stitches through the sides of the braid and working diagonally backwards and forwards across the braided strips.

10 Position the end of the rug so there is an equal number of rounds on each side. Taper the strips so the braid will become narrower and narrower, and finally push the narrow, pointed end into the previous round of the rug. Trim off the excess fabric and handsew in place on the wrong side.

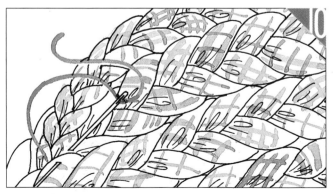

Useful Addresses

Curtain tracks,
poles and accessories
ARTISAN
4a Union Ct
20-22 Union Road
London SW4
England
Tel (0171) 498-6974

BYRON & BYRON
4 Hanover Yard
Noel Road
London N1
England
Tel (0171) 704-9290

MCKINNEY & CO
1 Wandon St
London SW6
England
Tel (0171) 384-1377

KIRSCH CO
PO Box 370
Sturges, MI 49091
USA
Tel 1-800-528-1407

SPRING WINDOWS
FASHIONS DIVISION
7549 Graber Rd
Middleton, WI 53562
USA
Tel 1-800-356-9102

Fabrics and trimmings
(mail order)
ANNA FRENCH
343 Kings Road
London SW3 5ES
England
Tel (0171) 351-1126
(Lace and patterned sheers)

BOROVICK FABRICS
16 Berwick St
London W1V 4HP
England
Tel (0171) 437-2180

MATERIAL WORLD
290 Battersea Park Road
London SW11 3BT
England
Tel (0181) 361-7888

BAER FABRICS
515 E Market St
Louisville, KY 40202
USA
Tel 1-800-769-7666 or (502) 583-5521

CALICO CORNERS
653 W Lancaster Ave
Strafford-Devon, PA 19087
USA
Tel (610) 688-1505

CLOTILDE, INC
2 S Smart Way
B-8031
Stevens Point, WI 54481
USA
Tel 1-800-772-2891

NANCY'S NOTIONS
PO Box 683
Beaver Dam, WI 53916-0683
USA
Tel 1-800-833-0690
or (414) 887-0391

Trimmings
G J TURNER & CO
(TRIMMINGS) LTD
Fitzroy House
Abbot St
London E8 3DP
England
Tel (0171) 254 -8187 (mail order)

V V ROULEAUX
10 Symons St
London SW3 8TJ
England
Tel (0171) 730-4413

WENDY CUSHING LTD
Chelsea Harbour
London SW10 OXE
England
Tel (0171) 351-5796

M & J TRIMMINGS
1008 Sixth Ave
New York, NY 10018
USA
(212) 391-9072

Specialist fabrics/accessories
AIR DE PROVENCE
Redhouse Farm
Eynsham Road
Botley, Oxford OX2 9NH
England
Tel (01865) 862442

APPALACHIA
14A George St
St Albans, Herts AL3 4ER
England
(Colonial accessories and fabrics)

CIEL DECOR
187 New Kings Road
London SW6
England
Tel (0171) 731-0444

COLEFAX & FOWLER
110 Fulham Road
London SW3 6RL
England
Tel (0181) 874-6484
(Country house style fabrics)

LAURA ASHLEY
Head Office
150 Bath Rd
Maidenhead, Berks SL6 4YS
England
Tel (01628) 39151
(country house and cottage style
fabrics and trimmings)

LUNN ANTIQUES
96 New Kings Road
London SW6 4LU
England
(antique textiles)

THE SHAKER SHOP
25 Harcourt St
London W1H 1DT
England
Tel (0171) 724-7672
(Shaker fabrics, furniture and
accessories)

LAURA ASHLEY
398 Columbus Ave
New York, NY 10024
Tel 1-800-847-0202
(country house and cottage style
fabrics and trimmings)

PIERRE DEUX
870 Madison Ave
New York, NY 10021
USA
Tel (212) 570-9343
(French country fabrics and
accessories)

Acknowledgements

The author would like to thank Panda Ribbons for supplying all the ribbons used in her projects, Coats Crafts UK for the bed linen embroidery on pages 89-91, The French Linen Co Ltd for the jacquard tea towels used on pages 92-3, and Air de Provence for the Provencal placemats on pages 76-7. Special thanks to Penny Hill and Beryl Miller.

PHOTOGRAPHIC CREDITS

The publishers wish to thank the following photographers and organizations for their kind permission to reproduce their photographs:

Front cover: Abode/Ian Parry.
Back cover: Robert Harding Syndication/IPC Magazines

Abode/Trevor Richards18/Ian Parry 20 & 82; Crowson Fabrics(Serendipity Festival) 96-7 (Serendipity & Mara) 100; Michael Freeman 112-3; Lars Hallen(Lebell House) 52-3; Robert Harding Syndication/IPC Magazines 2, 4, 8-9, 25, 34-5, 36, 41, 45, 64, 66, 67, 78-9, 81, 83, 85, 98, 101, 103; The Interior Archive/Christopher Simon Sykes 111/Fritz von Der Schulenburg 54, 61; David Phelps 21, 25, 56; Ianthe Ruthven 65, 119; Paul Ryan/International Interiors (Ann Robinson) 16-7, 38, 75(Marcel Wolterinck), 83(r), 99, 117 (Sasha Waddell); Elizabeth Whiting & Associates/Cote Sud 37, 48, 55, 80(l)/Michael Dunne 114/Neil Lorimer 69, 80(r)/ Peter Woloszynski 62-3.

All other photography by Mark Gatehouse.

Index

*Combining inspirational colour photographs with practical advice,
The Pleasures of Home series shows you how to decorate your home
in creative ways which reflect your own personality. Each chapter
deals with a particular room, decorated in a specific cultural or
historical style. While a different aspect of home decoration is covered
in each volume, the themes of the chapters are consistent across the
series, so that the books can be used together if desired. Whether you
would like guidelines on how to adapt the main features of each style
or step-by-step instructions and illustrations for particular projects,
you'll find all you need to know in* The Pleasures of Home.